I Can't
Date Jesus

I Can't Date Jesus

Love, Sex, Family, Race, and Other Reasons I've Put My Faith in Beyoncé

MICHAEL ARCENEAUX

ATRIA PAPERBACK

NEW YORK LONDON TORONTO SYDNEY NEW DELHI

ATRIA
PAPERBACK

An Imprint of Simon & Schuster, Inc.
1230 Avenue of the Americas
New York, NY 10020

Copyright © 2018 by Michael Arceneaux

First Atria Paperback edition July 2018

ATRIA PAPERBACK and colophon are trademarks of
Simon & Schuster, Inc.

For information about special discounts for bulk purchases,
please contact Simon & Schuster Special Sales at 1-866-506-1949 or
business@simonandschuster.com.

The Simon & Schuster Speakers Bureau can bring authors to
your live event. For more information or to book an event, contact
the Simon & Schuster Speakers Bureau at 1-866-248-3049 or visit
our website at www.simonspeakers.com.

Interior design by Dana Sloan

Manufactured in the United States of America

10 9 8 7 6 5 4 3 2

Library of Congress Cataloging-in-Publication Data is available.

ISBN 978-1-5011-7885-6
ISBN 978-1-5011-7886-3 (ebook)

Once an old high school classmate told me at the Pappadeaux's off of 610 in Houston that I would end up working at Burger King because I had majored in journalism.

This book is dedicated to dummies like that who don't know when to shut the hell up.

Also: pay fast food workers livable wages.

I know where I'm going and I know the truth, and
I don't have to be what you want me to be. I'm free
to be what I want.

—MUHAMMAD ALI

But in the long run, no matter what I do for
the rest of my life, I'll know I did something
wonderful by saying what I felt.

—FIONA APPLE

Contents

I Can't
Date Jesus

Introduction: **Where'd You Go?**

Before that day, I hadn't been to church in five Beyoncé albums. Well, not for service, anyway. In that span of time, I had stepped inside two separate churches for three funerals, but as my mama and most faithful churchgoers will promptly make clear, solely stepping into the House of the Lord isn't the same thing as attending mass or church service and truly engaging in praise and worship. Until that April morning, the closest I had come to church attendance was watching WeTV's *Mary Mary*, an eponymously titled reality series about that gospel duo, and body rolling to tracks of theirs like "God in Me." (But only the chopped-and-screwed versions, because as a native of Houston, Texas, everything sounds better to me chopped and screwed—jams for Jesus included.) Other quasi-religious activities for my church-less life included posting contemptuous social media updates about the Baptist church across the street from my Harlem apartment and how the incredibly bad singing coming out of it is disrespectful to Jesus. Even if I had become an estranged acquaintance of Jesus, I didn't feel He deserved

1

a shaky-vocals-having soloist and an equally terrible choir shouting off-key about Christ's love. If Jesus Christ was nailed to a cross in order to die for our sins, the least any church singers can do is find the correct note.

I often describe myself as a recovering Catholic, but when a more pointed question such as "So what do you believe in?" surfaces, I struggle with specificity.

I know that I am not an atheist. For me, to let go of the idea of God altogether would mean completely sinking to a level of cynicism and jadedness that could ultimately devour me whole. That is not to speak for atheists in general; it's merely what an embracement of atheism would mean for me. I cling to the idea that there has to be something bigger than us. Perhaps God is not, as He is so often depicted, the old white man with a white beard as long as a freshly sewn-in, twenty-two-inch Peruvian body-wave human-hair weave. Maybe God is not a man at all. Over time, I've grown weary of using male pronouns to denote that Divine Being. In all the years of my absence from "God's house," I have continued to fall to my knees— sometimes on a random sidewalk—to pray, if for no other reason than to leave some line of communication open. As for Jesus, I've swung back and forth from "That's my nigga!" to treating Him like a friend with whom I've fallen out because I hate a lot of His punk-ass friends (e.g., so many Christians) and never really had a proper sit-down with Him to make amends. Many with a firmer stance about their religion have mocked or at least expressed befuddlement at those who say they are more spiritual than religious. It is their belief that such a noncommittal position reads as lazy, like it's putting the tip in with respect to faith, but not really going all the way. For them, it's merely a matter of effort: *You can do it, put your back into it!*

Such opinions are a reflection of their own lack of will to step outside of themselves and their experiences and see how those on the other side feel. How can you be obedient to dogma you've found oppressive? How can you cling to tradition and exalt a vision of God that minimizes you and expects you to suppress what is innate to you? Is it not an exercise in futility to place your faith in a belief system that doesn't completely believe in you? Some of us either do not know the answers or have found ones that leave us on our own respective journeys for clarity and understanding, independent of any organized religion. It may not be a definitive position, but there are periods in life during which a gray area may be best. For those who do not understand or refuse to understand, such is their right. They also have the right to mind their own damn business.

Anyway, in the midst of this cloudiness over my religious ID, I found my way back inside of church to attend service. Naturally, I would go on Easter Sunday, one of three specific days when a bevy of lay Christians or full-fledged heathens opt to go check in with God. (The other two are Christmas and Mother's Day.) Funnily enough, there was no grandiose moment that got me back inside of a church for the first time in well over a decade. It was just a simple request from my best friend, andré (he prefers the aesthetic of lowercase lettering, and I respect it). dré and I were at brunch a week before and he asked me if I wanted to come to church with him on Easter.

I don't recall what number Bellini I was on, but I was of sober mind when I replied, "Sure."

Now, for years and years, my mother had been encouraging me to go back to church. The most opportune times for her to push her agenda were whenever I felt my lowest. My mother may not have always seen me as wholly as I would have liked, but she was one of the very few people who could see through my veneer, a person who knew that beneath the flexes of strength and feigned indifference to a hostile world was a man often struggling to hold it together. In these weak moments of mine, she would push me to go back to "God's house" to renew my faith and, by extension, be in a better place in every facet of my life. I liked my methods better: Mary J. Blige albums and maybe another prescription to a generic form of Celexa. After a while, she did take the hint that I was as firm in my choice not to go as she was in hers that I ought to. She would continue to encourage me to pray, send rosaries and prayer books, and sometimes casually mention that I might want to tip my toe into God's residence. But in time, she majorly fell back.

She wanted the best for me. She loved me. She just didn't understand that what she wanted for me was not for me. Her technique always made me think of this line from Pimp C on UGK's "Hi-Life": "Tired of hearing grandma telling me, 'When you gonna go to church, Chad?'"

dré was different in that he understood my conflicting feelings about religion based on my sexuality better than most did—even if he didn't handle them in the same way. He was a preacher's kid, but he was neither rebellious toward the faith nor didactic in how he discussed it with other people. As for the church he invited me to, First Corinthian Baptist Church in Harlem, I had heard about it and its well-regarded pastor, Michael A. Walrond Jr.—better known as "Pastor Mike"—repeatedly since I had moved to Harlem some four years prior. Despite constantly hearing about how great he was, I had never received a direct invitation from him to see for myself.

So when dré actually did extend a direct invitation, I accepted and went to church with him the following week.

I grew up Catholic, so a lot of traditions associated with the Black church were much different from what I was used to. For example, I could just as easily have worn jeans as I did slacks if I went to church. Outside of major holidays, I never had to dress to impress anyone at the Catholic churches in Houston that I attended. I simply just needed to be present. And one thing I did like about Catholicism was that Catholics were big fans of brevity. A typical mass was no longer than an hour, and even on holidays like Easter and Christmas, it extended to no more than ninety minutes. On the other hand, my only other recollection of attending a Baptist service was being in church for what felt like an entire weekend.

Thankfully, dré explained to me that I could wear denim and a button-up and that the nine-thirty service wasn't going to be too long because there was another one at eleven thirty. He and a few of his friends casually referred to the eleven-thirty service as "thot service." I'm not entirely sure why—I'm assuming because it's the latest service and catered to the night owls who needed a bit more time to recover from the previous evening—but all I knew was that it was the longest service so absolutely not the one for me. Two hours of church service sounds like two-for-one mass to this old Catholic. Nope.

I actually got to church before dré, and he found me in line to get in. There were two separate lines: one was for regular parishioners, most of whom were Black, and the other one was largely for white European tourists. It looked like segregation, only the So So Def remix in which Black people had decidedly more power over the space. I would later find out that there were plenty of Black tourists in the same line as I was, but the optics were striking all the same. While waiting to be let inside, I came across a media legend whose work I'd long admired and whom I knew socially. He showed visible shock when he made eye contact with me, then came up to me and quipped, "Oh, honey, don't burn the church down." Ah, a joke with a tablespoon of judgment: I was indeed back to church. *Praise the Lord*. At least he hadn't greeted me with "Fancy seeing you here, fornicator."

Clearly rusty on how to enter a church, much less one of this size, I grabbed my wallet and was about to pull out my ID to show it to the usher that stood before the doors. Yes, as if he were a club bouncer. Yes, as if I were trying to get in free before eleven and rush to the bar to enjoy that two-for-one drinks special. I believe God has a sense of humor, so I'd like to think He saw that moment and said, "This ridiculous, bird-ass bitch."

Once I stepped inside the sprawling, gorgeous space, I marveled at its beauty, but the images that stuck with me most were of the people sitting inside. I saw a woman that I knew was married to another woman. Directly behind me was another gay man I knew. I ended up sitting between two gay men. All of them were regular attendants, yet none of them appeared torn about being there. Of course, there have always been gays, lesbians, bisexuals, and trans people inside churches, but although their talent might be on display in, like, say, the choir, their sexuality was far less pronounced. As in, don't ask, don't tell, just sing your lil' gay self off for God. And, indeed, I did clock plenty o' gays in the First Corinthian choir. But this felt different from what I was accustomed to. I knew what it was like to be around Christians who knew of my sexuality but who merely tolerated me. ("Tolerated" meaning they knew I was gay but avoided the subject at all costs. There was a difference between being *welcomed* and being *tolerated*.) Here, everyone—and I mean everyone—seemed to be welcomed and behaved as such. In the front row, which was reserved for other pastors of the church, I saw a sea of women. Women were typically marginalized out of leadership roles in the church. In Catholicism, no such roles even existed. But here, on this day and in this church, there were more women pastors than there were male pastors.

When Pastor Mike spoke, I understood quickly why so many people had fawned over him for so long. With respect to various members of the clergy, having read the Bible didn't mean you actually understood it. There was memorization and repetition, and then there was comprehension.

During service, they called on those who were visitors to stand; I did so reluctantly. Toward the end, they called on those who wanted to join the church to step down and approach the altar. I kept my Black ass in my seat. *Let's not get ahead of ourselves, saints.*

I ended up interviewing Pastor Mike for a work-related project a few weeks later. I asked him why LGBTQ*SWV* folks felt so welcomed (I added SWV to honor both the girl group and the expanding identities; I'm also a smartass). He said it was because they *were* welcomed. That he was not condemning who they were. That he had not been placed in that pulpit to make them feel less-than or like an affront to God. He also agreed with what I meant about many people in the clergy not necessarily being theologians and thus having a limited understanding of the text they were supposed to be teaching to parishioners. Biblical literalists of convenience irked the living hell out of me, I told him. We both likened the situation to various cable pundits who didn't know so much about policy but were adept at repetition and talking points.

Seeing how moved I had been during the service, one of dré's friends suggested that I write about it. As a freelance writer, the constant essay-hustling had me always in a state of planning for the sake of a paycheck. But that was not why I had come, so I brushed the idea off. I had gone simply because I had been invited, I told him. In hindsight, the invitation had come at the time when I was truly ready to accept it. After service, dré and I hopped in an Uber to join friends for brunch. I told dré that I had enjoyed my time there and that I would go back. But I made clear that I wasn't joining the church.

Frankly, while I *had* enjoyed my time there, in terms of what I believed in—or, in my case, didn't believe in—nothing changed. There was no moment that compelled me to reenter a relationship with Christianity. It felt good, but not that good. What I will say, though, is that what I saw at First Corinthian in Harlem was the Christianity I wish I had had as a child, as a teenager, and as a young man trying to find a place in a world that appeared unwilling to offer one. This was the Jesus I had needed to see back then. These were the Christians I had needed much earlier in my life. Maybe if I had found a church and pastor like this, my views on religion might be different. Perhaps questions about the state of my Christianity wouldn't require me to first locate a feather duster. Yes, I was moved by what I had seen and heard, but I had already moved beyond needing a church and a member of the clergy to guide me to God or define my sense of what's right and wrong. In those years of separation, I created my own idea of who God is and what God means to me. The same goes for my moral compass. I've become a solo act when it comes to how I process things and what spirituality now looks like—and I'm wary of walking back to the old band whose validation I have long moved past requiring, as I simply do not need it.

Months later, someone from Saint Mark the Evangelist, the church I attended regularly as a child, with whom I went to catechism (think vacation Bible school for Baptists or the weird thing they do for entry-level Scientologists), reached out to me via Facebook. She had watched an interview in which I described myself as a "recovering Catholic." She told me, "Michael, you have me in tears with your video post. I had no idea you felt that way about being Catholic. It really hurt to hear you say you were recovering from it." She went on to tell me that she understood where I was coming from, and she shared a story about her guilt over perceived faults she had committed in the past. These "faults," though, were simply the acts of a woman with autonomy over her body. Not abortion (not that it matters) but a medical procedure that she would later learn was considered to be a sin. She spoke of extreme depression as a result of the guilt stemming from her decision, but, ultimately, a priest told her during confession that she had already been forgiven, that she merely needed to forgive herself. She told me this as a means of reaching out to me and to let me know that I "[didn't] have to feel that way about the Catholic Church." She described the church as a big family; that we all had different opinions yet we loved each other. And that the church we both grew up in was different now. That it was welcoming, and that she could actually "see and feel the love."

She made it sound a lot like First Corinthian. Unfortunately, her telling me this story did not warm me back to the Catholic Church or any church. All she did was remind me of what had kept me away for so long. When she admitted that she continued to feel guilty after all this time, I told her therein lay the problem: there had never been any reason for her to feel guilty. She told me that I could be a "returning Catholic" and be "free of guilts," but she wasn't even free from hers. Her efforts were well intentioned but not at all convincing. I didn't doubt her when she said our church had changed, but I had long ago decided not to wait for any individual church or institution to change. To put the fate of my sanity in either was too great a risk. I needed to find my own moral compass. I needed to develop my own understanding of my place in the world and my right to be exactly who I was and how that related to God. To do it on my own was a far more difficult task, but the time away had made me much more comfortable with myself.

This book is about unlearning every damaging thing I've seen and heard about my identity and allowing myself the space to figure out who I am and what that means on my terms. I may not have figured every single thing out, but I do know the stories I heard as a child and the damnation assigned to me because of my identity no longer haunt me. I do know that I am a good person. Most of all, I know that God gave us the gift of discernment and that I've made the most out of it. I'm glad that I did not merely give in to deference because it may have very well been the death of me. Being able to step back inside of a church that truly lived up to Christian virtues was refreshing, but I am reminded by another openly homophobic church only a few blocks away from where I live now that this is still not the case for all. The same can be said of a childhood friend being stricken with the level of guilt only a religious institution can instill.

Still, for a brief moment on Easter Sunday 2017, fifteen years after essentially abandoning Christianity in an act of self-preservation, I was able to experience it the way I wish I always had. I do not know what my future with religion looks like. I don't see myself becoming saved by forty and releasing a trap gospel album soon after, but stranger things have happened. Whatever does happen, though, I know that, with or without it, I'll be fine. If it can boost my life, great; but if it not, I'll at least continue giving Jesus the courtesy of condemning anyone who can't sing for Him in the correct key. Amen.

The First Taste

"**S**hh, be quiet! If they hear us, we'll get in trouble."

That's what five-year-old me whispered to the boy in the cot next to mine. I don't remember his name, but I'll never forget the feeling he gave me. He was tickling me, which sounds innocent on the surface, but the spots on my body where he attempted to tickle me made it anything but. Typically, you tickle someone to make them squirm for the sake of laughter. Yet the touching felt tantalizing, its intentions different. So was my reaction. We may have snickered as we touched each other, but it wasn't so much comical as it was two little boys letting their curiosity get the best of them and enjoying a new and perplexing but nonetheless exciting feeling.

I've never been one to nap, which meant that I spent much of the designated nap time at daycare doing something else. And that something else usually centered on an inappropriate touchy-feely game with other boys. I can't even recall how the game began. It just sort of did. And, obviously, I had a favorite boy with whom I'd play the game.

Fun came at a price, however, if you were caught. Such was the case for two other boys who had once been spotted moving a wee bit too feverishly underneath the covers. I couldn't see exactly what they were doing, since they were a few feet away, but I could make out the laughter that came as a result of it. Apparently, so could one of the daycare workers. After hovering over them for a minute or so, she quickly ordered them both to rise and follow her—no doubt to call their respective parents.

I once faced a similar scenario after I was caught behind the playground near the air conditioner pulling my pants down in front of another boy, who soon followed suit. It was like show-and-tell: the remix. Mrs. Rhodes, who ran the daycare, was not impressed with our take on that familiar pastime, however.

Once Mrs. Rhodes found us, it didn't take long for the tears to flow from my eyes, so afraid was I of what was coming next. I knew that I had enjoyed what I was doing, but I also knew that others— namely my parents—wouldn't share my enthusiasm. So, I opted to make myself look as pathetic as possible in hopes of being granted mercy: I cried every drop I could get out in order to prevent Mrs. Rhodes from telling my mother I had misbehaved. With such natural acting ability on display, it's no wonder Mrs. Harris would later cast me in the lead role of the play *Lil' Red Goes to the Hood* a few years later. As a child, I had the reputation of being sneaky in my family. I personally didn't think of myself as sneaky, but everything I just described was some sneaky shit. Perhaps a little manipulative to boot. The goal was simply to not get a whupping or be put on punishment. That near chance of my mom finding out just what I was doing on her dime at daycare spooked me—but it still was not enough to suppress my burgeoning curiosity. Instead, I was just more careful and a lot less audible.

Sometimes I debate whether I'm violating child pornography laws while recalling my own childhood, but none of my actions were really all that different from those of the other kids who played "doctor." This was the same game, only with a same-sex spin. Besides, kids of opposite sexes got in trouble for getting frisky with each other too. We were all a little inquisitive, and hell, *Barney & Friends* was boring. I did try my nap-time shenanigans with a girl once. It was about as much fun as singing along to a dancing purple dinosaur.

As a young adult, I read an interview that Janet Jackson gave to the now defunct *Blender* magazine in 2004. In it, she discussed having a sense of her sexuality very early. "As I've gotten older, I've come to realize that I had a very active sexual mind at a very young age," she explained. "I hope that doesn't sound bad." She went on to add, "When you're a kid, you have little fantasies, but I saw myself being with Barry Manilow as an adult, not as a kid."

So, while Janet is a better singer (shut up, she can sing), dancer, and recording artist (sadly my rap career remains a figment of my imagination) than me, I can confidently claim that my taste in men might be superior, 'cause, girl, Barry Manilow? Who fantasizes about Barry Manilow, besides middle-aged moms who can't clock their fellow queens? And just picture an adult Janet Jackson having sex with Barry Manilow. Actually, don't—especially if you wear contact lenses, as that would be a waste of a perfectly good pair. *Diff'rent Strokes* indeed, sis. Thanks to that interview, though, I realized that I wasn't some loose kindergartner. I was just exploring my natural urges like Janet had. I'm like Janet but before the Super Bowl.

I've never been able to find a space in which I could talk about these events that felt free of judgment or presumption. No, I was never molested. Yes, every boy back then was a willing participant. Why was I doing it? I'm not sure, but it happened. I don't regret it.

Still, back then I had no name to call these feelings that I had for other boys. At that time in my life, I had not yet heard labels like "gay," "bisexual," or "queer." It took the death of a relative from a then controversial disease to both enlighten and terrify me. And the term that did awaken was a slur that has stayed with me for much of my life.

—

I don't remember much about my uncle Daniel. I've never been particularly close to my dad's side of the family, as he never has been either. I have no recollection of what my paternal grandfather looked like, and while I would see some of his brothers and sisters, depending on the year and the holiday, I remember nothing about Daniel. Not a single thing other than how he died.

My sole memory of him is seeing him at peace during his funeral mass at Saint Francis Xavier in Houston, on Reed Road. It was not my home church, but it was one of the few that remained predominantly Black, and was near my paternal grandmother's house. No side of my family started in Texas. They all came from Louisiana, and with them the Catholic faith most of them were raised in. Many would come here, then as adults go off and turn to a Christian denomination better suited for them. And there, inside that quaint Catholic Church, I accompanied my mother to the front of the altar and started to sob hysterically after looking into Daniel's open casket. Yes, I had cried at the daycare to get myself out of trouble, but

I typically hated crying, in general. To be fair, though, I was a child standing before a corpse. I seized the moment.

My mother was the one who later explained his death to me. She told me that my uncle, her brother-in-law, had died of something called AIDS. With it being only 1990 and drugs having ravaged the Black community throughout much of the previous decade, his death signaled an opportunity to instill a valuable lesson in me: don't be like Daniel, the heroin addict. See where drugs can lead you.

My dad didn't want me to be like Daniel either, though he said so in another way: "Fuck that faggot."

He was in the midst of a drunken stupor. The kind that went on and on into the night until he finally decided to shut up, go to his bed, and stay in it.

My mom: "Don't listen to him, Michael. Daniel wasn't gay."

I always took my mother's word over my father's, but something seemed amiss about what she said in comparison to what he was screaming about. She didn't sound like she really believed what she was saying. She seemed uncomfortable, as if she had something to hide. Say, the truth that my dead uncle probably contracted AIDS from gay sex, sharing needles, or some combination of the two.

So the truth needed to be scaled back a bit. I was a child, after all. There was only so much my inquisitive but young mind could probably grapple with. So perhaps with my benefit in mind, she explained death in much tamer terms. It was easier for the both of us that way.

Yet my father's screams of "faggot" only intensified as that night went on. Those screams are what I'll never forget. That slur is what will always hit me in the pit of my stomach.

"Faggot!"

"Faggot!"

"Faggot!"

And on and on he went about what a faggot his dead brother was. The reasons why my uncle had never come around became clearer.

My father had a habit of disclosing information about a given person or situation he otherwise opted to forgo discussing whenever he had too much beer and brown liquor. This is how I discovered what it meant to be different and how some people might react to it. More important, this is how I learned how being different could lead to your demise.

"I told you about sex when you were three," my mother once explained to me matter-of-factly. This made perfect sense, because, even as a very young child, I couldn't recall a time when I didn't understand the mechanics of sex—or, at the very least, the context of where babies came from. My mom may have been a devout Catholic, but she was also a registered nurse who took care of new mothers. Sex was a fact of life, so she made sure I knew about it. Nevertheless, it wasn't until Daniel, and my dad's tirade, that I learned that when two people of the same sex touched each other, it could lead to death. Moreover, no matter how you were, there was certain behavior that could ostracize you—even from those that were your own blood.

Those lessons were ingrained in me traumatically, and they only got worse as I aged and began to hear other words like "sissy" and "punk." They all meant the same thing. They all made me trace myself back to those cots and what I had done in them underneath the covers. They all made me petrified. The same went for religion, which became further indoctrinated in me over time.

As a result of all this, the games I used to play had to stop.

———

The older I got, the more pressed I became about "beating it." It was so much easier said than done. For starters, I couldn't even masturbate to girls. Visions of Janet Jackson's dancer Omar Lopez were far more stimulating than the thought of Miss Jackson herself. My young penis didn't seem to care how nasty she was. Lil' Kim's infamous promotional poster for her debut album, *Hardcore*, where she squatted in a leopard bikini, did not have the same effect on me as the rapper Ma$e did. Or Silkk the Shocker. And definitely not Will Smith, any hour on any given day of the week.

I fought and I fought. I would lie in bed so many times telling myself, "Think of a woman! Think of a woman!" It would work a few times, but mainly my dick would turn into Play-Doh in protest.

This essentially set the tone for failure after failure with girls from K–12.

Things started off with Jessica, who assaulted me with her jacket as a means of declining my advances en route to recess. She was lucky I didn't bite her with my buckteeth. Mean lil' heifer. With Lucy, I approached her in a way that nixed the chance of a zipper scratching my eye socket. I passed the classic note: "Do you like me: Yes or no? Circle one." Lucy wrote back, "I like you a lot but only as a friend."

In truth, most of the girls only liked me as a friend. No one had the language to write back, "Nigga, you gay." Or "Beloved, you're a homosexual." Or, "Sis, stop this."

In middle school, I was fat and growing tits as fast as the girls were. Nothing happened. Bless my heart.

I didn't manage to have my first date with a girl until I was seventeen. I met Camille through a mutual friend, Nicole. Even though I had my license, I was not the best driver. Camille noticed this very early into our date. Fearing for her life, she offered a suggestion that came across as more like a demand: let her drive. Being a gentleman without any money to settle the multimillion-dollar wrongful death suit her parents might have filed, I obliged. The date went okay for a boy who clearly liked other boys and was awkward as hell around women in romantic settings. That is, until we reached the part where I—the guy—was supposed to make a move. See, what had happened was . . . I thought to do something but couldn't follow through. Not even because we had both just eaten at a Chinese buffet and neither of us was packing a mint. I was too intimidated and not interested enough to overcome my anxiety. Instead, I shook her hand.

Smooth!

I never heard from Camille again.

There was also a girl who had the same last name as mine. My last name is semicommon in Houston and very common across Louisiana, so the chances of us being related were likely. I tried to convince myself otherwise. She didn't like me in the end. It was for the best: I have no idea why I was trying to act out a *Game of Thrones* incest prequel.

Another girl by the name of Reese didn't want to be my girlfriend, but she randomly yet graciously offered to help in another way. We were sitting in pre–AP chemistry and she was explaining to me how some football player had had the audacity to fuck her with his socks still on. Since I was a virgin, I assumed maybe his feet were merely cold. Sensing my naïveté, she pressed to see whether or not I had had sex yet. After I blurted out no, she quipped, "Oh, but you're so cute. I'll fuck you, Michael."

As appreciative as I was for her offer of a mercy fuck, I declined. If I couldn't even force myself to try and kiss a girl on a date, I definitely wasn't ready to kiss another's crotch. I was beginning to think my curiosity about women had peaked when I still had my baby teeth.

That is, until I met Alicia. She was by far the most beautiful girl I ever tried to pursue. Years later she would go on to be a professional cheerleader for an NFL team. She was so gorgeous that I'm certain she could've landed one of the players as a husband had she put her mind and her walls to it. At one point I believed I loved her. I believed it because for once I didn't have to force myself to be into her.

With these feelings came the idea that maybe, just maybe, I finally had a real shot at overcoming my nagging attraction to guys— including her ex-boyfriend.

I wanted to make this work, so I did everything I could to try and get Alicia to like me back. For all my efforts, I felt as if she was into me, though for one reason or another it felt like she was ashamed about it. I wasn't sure why, exactly, but that was always my sneaking suspicion about her. Whatever it was, my feelings for her soured after she stood me up the day of the TRL Tour.

Not only was it disrespectful to me but it was also offensive to the star of the show: Beyoncé. Who stands up Beyoncé? A damn fool. Making matters worse, Alicia was my ride! My mother was using a rental while her car was in the shop. She didn't feel comfortable letting me drive the rented car with my name not being on the insurance. That, and she presumably knew I was lying when I said someone had hit the car when, in actuality, my terrible-driving ass had hit something. In my defense, my friend Kim had reassured me that I could make that turn. She was wrong. So wrong.

Without a date and minus a ride, I frantically called everyone I knew, hoping I could find someone willing to be my chauffeur and guest in exchange for gas money and the chance to bask in Beyoncé's greatness with me.

In hindsight, my known devotion to Beyoncé might have been why I wasn't having much luck with girls. At a hood-as-all-hell high school in a neighborhood where most of the boys' musical palettes dealt with subject matter involving "swangin' and bangin'," it probably wasn't the smartest move to note that while you did have an affinity for Southern rap, you could easily shift gears and sing along with the girls who bashed about bugaboos and boasted about being too bootylicious for you, babe.

Even after all of this, I continued my pursuit of Alicia. After the seventh or so blow off, though, I bought a clue, gave up, and placed myself on an indefinite break from dating girls. It just seemed fruitless: I couldn't get myself to kiss a girl or have sex with one when she offered, and I failed at securing the heart of the one girl I had managed to care somewhat for without force.

By the end of high school girls were as intriguing to me as they had been on that cot more than a decade earlier. On top of that, for all the girls I pursued, there were probably at least two boys whom I found far more interesting. As a result, like many a gay, I used the Internet to vaguely explore an unshakable feeling. And through AOL Instant Messenger, Yahoo Messenger, and the private sections of far too many message boards, I did the virtual equivalent of what

I used to do in those cots during nap time. I tried to look at women in porn too, but arousal always required far more effort in comparison to feelings that were always innate and urgent.

But while I was ready to finally give up on my pursuit of girls, I was not ready to go beyond that and finally move beyond adolescent sexual explorations with boys into a tangible same-sex encounter. I was physically ready for it, but mentally I was still caught up in the trauma of my childhood and the religion that told me that such a thing was an aberration of God's natural order.

—

The way I was introduced to what it meant to be gay never left me. The death that seemed certain to come with it. That immediate resentment you were sure to face over it. None of that had been shaken yet. It didn't help that pop culture—the only point many of us have in which to see our true selves—offered no images that I could relate to growing up, and nothing that could lift me out of the dark side of the life that I experienced early.

So all I knew was the death of Uncle Daniel, the death of Pedro Zamora from *The Real World,* and the death of Andrew Beckett from the film *Philadelphia.* The only living images I could think of were Blaine Edwards and Antoine Merriweather, whose skits on *In Living Color* offered portrayals of gay Black men that were cartoonish and buffoonish in nature. The same can be said of the author J. L. King, who helped spread the myth of the "down-low brother" that gave *all of the women the AIDS* with his secret gay rendezvous on an episode of *The Oprah Winfrey Show.*

All the while, there wasn't sex ed in schools explaining to me that so long as I protected myself, I would be fine. The same went for what to actually do with these feelings and the mechanics behind them. I only knew what I had seen. And what I had seen was frightening and alienating.

So I just did me: literally. I thought of members of the track team—or, rather, every track team I had ever seen on TV. I thought of multiple rappers, singers, and actors. I thought of people I basically cyber-hoed with on IM. Every once in a while, I'd push myself to make my penis rise at the thought of a woman. Eh.

Masturbation was also considered a sin, but I rationalized my actions by telling myself that as long as I kept touching my own penis instead of someone else's, God wouldn't grab Moses's staff and knock the shit out of me with it. And T-Boz of TLC once released a promasturbation single entitled "Touch Myself." It flopped everywhere else but on my personal CD player, and as a result, I relied on my right hand to keep me from living what I thought was the wrong way. The decision to sin as a solo artist, to oppose exploring my sexuality in more tangible ways, spurred unneeded misery for years to come. It only stunted my development and made me more anxious—and, by extension, occasionally awkward around men.

It's often said that knowing who you are, or at the very least possessing a sneaking suspicion of such early in life, is a blessing. The people who share this sentiment need to write it on a piece of paper, ball it up, and then proceed to pour barbecue sauce all over it as they eat it. Early self-awareness is a blessing only if who you are comes with a support system and an education. If you don't have those, it's easy to find yourself feeling stuck and sullen. I learned a certain part of my identity very early, but it was met with a near-instant confirmation of how unwelcome that part of my identity was to those surrounding me.

I liked everything much better before all of this happened. When the look of a cute boy wasn't soiled by the sight of a man in a casket, condemnation for his actions afterward, warnings of fire and brimstone, and images all conveying abnormality.

That's why it was so easy for an innocent tickle to turn into something that taunted me far longer than it should have.

That's why it was so easy to end up afraid.

I wish I had been more daring. I don't like how long it took me to embrace who I was. I hate thinking that what happened to me at six stopped me from being the best ho I could be in my teens and twenties. I try not to live with regret, but it's difficult not to reflect on what might've been every so often. But I have also learned that we deal with what we can how we can until we get better. It took longer than it should have to deal with my past because where I come from, we tend to let things linger and fester. We bottle things up until it eats us inside. Sometimes we rupture in rage. Other times we turn to vices to bury the pain from whatever images and events feel unshakable despite the irony of us never confronting them head-on.

It was not the correct way, but it was the only way I knew until I was able to develop greater nerve and take greater control of my own destiny and challenge what all had been instilled in me. I longed for the moment when I could be with another guy in the dark, lie there, and *play* in peace. For all my fears about intimacy and death, what was really destroying me all that time was trying to live a lie. Something had to give.

I See a Priest in You

I learned to bow down to big baby Jesus early in life. My mother, a devout Catholic, had given my brother and me kid-themed Bibles to read, biblical cartoons on VHS to watch, and plenty of other religious-themed material to keep us abreast of all things Christ Our Lord. When I say "biblical cartoons," I mean exactly what it sounds like: I used to watch animated depictions like one centered on, say, Adam and Eve from the book of Genesis. Yeah, that adorable story about the time God created humanity and let us frolic around Earth butt-naked with friendly wildebeests or whatever until his second human creation, Eve, couldn't keep her hands to herself and ate the fruit God had directly instructed her not to touch, as if it were His labeled lunch in the office refrigerator. The creators of these cartoons managed to leave out the way in which stories like these were used to subjugate women and promote patriarchy throughout history. Sure, the cartoons were just fine if you were into age-appropriate forms of indoctrination, but the storytelling and graphics were much sharper on *Chip 'n Dale: Rescue Rangers, G.I. Joe*, and *DuckTales* (*Ah-woo-ooh!*).

As for the "religious-themed material," I'm referring to various cards depicting noted saints such as Saint Michael the Archangel, Saint Pio of Pietrelcina, and Saint Martin de Porres (the Jackie Robinson of Saints, y'all), among many, many others. These were akin to baseball cards. On the front, you would see an image with the respective saint doing something he was best known for. For example, the card with Saint Michael featured him over the image of Lucifer, whose ass God commanded Mike-Mike to drop-kick out of heaven. Saint Martin de Porres appeared solemn and Black on his card. Imagine a box of Uncle Ben's rice, only with Ben looking sad because he knows he's about to consume so many carbs and summer is coming.

Of all the prayers I read on those cards, it was Saint Michael's prayer I remember best:

Saint Michael the Archangel, defend us in battle;
be our protection against the wickedness and snares of the devil.
May God rebuke him, we humbly pray;
And do you, O prince of the heavenly host,
by the power of God,
thrust into hell Satan and all other evil spirits
who wander through the world seeking the ruin of souls.
Amen.

When I was a child, my mom used to say that I was named after Saint Michael and Saint Joseph. (Indeed, my middle name is Joseph.) Several years later, my sister told a different story: "You were named after Michael Jackson," she said. Apparently, Mom had initially wanted me to be named after my dad, which would have made me Wilton Jr. But my dad hated his first name, and no one ever called him that. His middle name was Joseph, and to this day, I've still only ever heard him known as Joe, Joe-Joe, or Doc. My sister, nine years older than I, was eventually tasked with helping name me, and being a huge fan of the Jacksons, she took inspiration from them.

"I almost told them to name you Randy Jackson."

I love my sister so much, but we would not be as tight as we are if my name were Randy Arceneaux and I learned she was responsible for that act of inhumanity. While it seems that Miss Janet authorizes only Randy Jackson to speak to the press on her behalf, I deserve better than being named after a spare Jackson. I also don't want to share a name with the *American Idol* judge who abuses the colloquial usage of "dawg." He's a nice guy, but no. Besides, the only desirable Randy I've ever seen was Randy from *Home Improvement*, but he was white and probably grew up to be a Trump supporter. Regardless of where my name came from, my mom made sure religion had an overall dominance over us, and whatever access point she could find to talk more about religion, she would exploit. In addition to the religious cartoons and saint-focused cards, I was also given an idea of how players on the other team operated. Dr. Marlena Evans provided the most memorable example: my mom had my brother and me watch *Days of Our Lives* during the period in which the main character, Marlena, was possessed by a demon; my mom clearly felt that this would teach us about the bad spirits roaming the earth. So throughout this soap-opera saga, I got an idea of what happens when the devil gets a hold of you. (Similarly, I got an early preview of one of God's most unfortunate creations: a bug-a-boo. Seriously, why was Stefano DiMera so damn pressed? Why couldn't the bastard just accept that Marlena didn't want him? He was rich and ready to trick. Were there no other attractive blonde women around who could give him what he so desperately wanted? If not for him and his pursuit of her, Marlena would've never had a demonic freak living in her body rent-free.)

Apparently, there were demons and bug-a-boos all around, so we needed protection. One method of protection came in the form of a scapular. A scapular is essentially two small pieces of cloth connected by a string that's worn like a necklace, only inside of your clothes. As it was explained to me, the Blessed Virgin Mary assured believers that "whoever dies clothed in this scapular shall not suffer eternal fire." That's right—when it's time to check into the gates of heaven, all scapular wearers have to do is flash that bad boy in front of Saint Peter as if it's a VIP wristband, and *bam,* they're in there. If a scapular helped boost my chances of strolling into heaven like George Jefferson moving on up to the East Side, do you think a demon was going to be able to shimmy into me on Earth? Mhmm.

I never took my scapular off. A lifelong klutz, I even showered with it on, because I was convinced I was going to slip and fall in there. No way was I going to risk dying in the shower and end up waiting in the general-admission line for admittance into heaven or end up like Marlena Evans. Plus, from what I had gathered through other required viewing in my home—those various Nostradamus-centered doomsday specials that NBC used to air, for example—we were only one bad person away from Armageddon. All that was left between us and fire on Earth was the third Antichrist attaining maximum power. Additional protection included getting on my knees every night and reciting my Our Father, Hail Mary, Glory Be, and Act of Contrition, not to mention my prayers to Saint Michael the Archangel and, of course, the Christian child's bedtime prayer, "Now I Lay Me Down to Sleep." I regularly attended Catholicism's answer to Sunday school—catechism—which paved the way to my first communion and ultimately my confirmation, which was me making the choice to enter the church of my own accord.

Yeah, when you're basically house-trained for well over a decade into a religion and a certain way of life, it's totally free will by the time you decide to join the church at sixteen or seventeen.

With my mother being so religious, you went to church every Sunday and every day that the Catholic Church had designated a holy day of obligation. There really was no other way to be. Well, there was my father, who stopped going to church years before I was born. His Sunday ritual consisted of going outside and popping open a couple of baker's dozens of beers while playing James Brown, Johnnie Taylor, 2Pac, and other CDs he picked out of my sister's car (he was partial to Master P's *Ghetto D* album) as he screamed to random people about whatever he felt was going wrong in his life. He had a better song selection than the organist at church, but his version of spirituality didn't seem all that rewarding.

By the age of eighteen, I could recall missing mass only once— and even then, I, along with my brother and sister, had to get permission to do so. The reason we were given a pass was because it was a storm so significant, even by Houston standards, that it made no sense to go out with all that rain and all that thundering and lightning.

Over time, my interest in my faith grew beyond "I don't really have much of a choice, now, do I?" I wanted to be more engaged, albeit for my own selfish reasons. Jesus was almost sold to me like a bit of a superhero (those cartoon depictions might have had something to do with that), leading me to think that he could do anything for me so long as I was persistent. All it would take was a lot of prayer. This premise worked perfectly for me, because I had so many requests for my super-duper savior. First, I wanted Jesus to get my father to curtail his drinking, which only made his character more choleric and, in turn, more susceptible to rage sessions that could turn violent. My request was based on the working theory that if he would calm the hell down, my mother would be far less stressed and kinder to her kids. He loved us, but the trauma he carried tormented all of us. Mom, of course, loved us, but she carried her own difficult past too. She was loving, though not always nice.

Another appeal to Jesus was for some more money to go around. My parents made sure we were clothed and fed, and definitely went above and beyond to get us many of the things I nagged them for (cable, so I could watch professional wrestling pay-per-view events; a Sega Genesis; a CD player, even if not the preferred brand—a very bratty thing of me to think back then), but by the time I got to middle school, I realized what others were provided, and this had me beginning to look at Jesus in terms of *gimmie-gimmie-gimmie, please, son of God*. I did go from wearing the same pairs of Wrangler jeans in middle school that got me mocked by some to Tommy Hilfiger and Polo by high school, so praise be to Jesus, a summer job, and my big sister swooping in to help me out.

But one of the bigger, far less successful requests from me to Jesus was to cure me. As I got older and gays grew in visibility, the Catholic Church and much of their Protestant brethren were becoming increasingly critical of homosexuals, their homosexual ways, and how homosexuals and their homosexual ways were spurring God's stress levels to bounce all across the universe.

Such criticism was never lost on me—me, who couldn't help but notice this incredibly cute boy to the right of me. And his younger brother too. Whew.

I knew early in life that I was drawn to boys more than to girls, but I learned just as early how such ways were frowned upon. What I had seen, heard, and learned haunted me. I wanted to change, and the only person I knew who could help me do so was Jesus. I convinced myself that he was going change me. Make me better. And by "better," I mean "straight." I was confident that it was going to happen. All I had to do was keep praying and wait. I was practically a walking commercial for those gay-be-gone groups who sing about the virtues of conversion therapy.

I didn't know it then, but in hindsight I can see that I was more in love with the idea of Jesus than anything else. Plus, I wasn't that good of a pal to Jesus. At first, Jesus was like that kid your mama forced you to play with. The kind you were initially indifferent to but then suddenly fawned over once you selfishly realized what they might be able to do for you. At the time, I thought I would do anything for Jesus because he was going to do everything for me eventually—at least so long as I kept pestering him about it while being a good Christian. The relationship was transactional yet substantive at the same time, because I needed to believe in someone better than everyone around me. I needed to believe things would get better. However, when met with the proposition of taking a more defined role in my religion and in church, I met it with equal parts befuddlement and resistance.

That proposition came in the form of me being recruited for the priesthood.

—

Yes, a priest scouted me, and, when the opportunity presented itself, he hit me with a sales pitch on why I ought to consider making a white collar a permanent staple of my wardrobe. The priest in question was named Father Martin, or "Father Marty," as he preferred to be called. He was an ex-Methodist music teacher turned Catholic priest. He was an older man, but there was something youthful to him if you looked beyond his not-so-believable curly wig. That wig! It wasn't a Jheri curl, because there were never any stains on his priest robes, but there were aesthetic similarities. Call it a second cousin of a Jheri curl who didn't want to look as juicy. It was the perfect wig to wear if you were heading to a Rick James–themed costume party.

Questionable tonsorial decisions notwithstanding, Father Marty was quite likable. He also made church a lot more interesting. When most Black folks discovered that I was Catholic, their immediate reaction was, "Catholic mass is so boring." That's rude as fuck, but can I spot the lie? Not really. Catholic masses are very much about ritual, but many of those rituals and the performances of them are very Eurocentric. The pageantry is beautiful and traditional, but traditional for whom? This is why so many Black Catholics went for the Protestants, whose services had far more pop to them. Perhaps being an ex-Methodist helped inform Father Marty's perspective, in that he could see swaths of Black people at Saint Mark the Evangelist Catholic Church who were present but not totally present in the current setup of mass there. That led Father Marty to help usher in a gospel choir, which livened up mass alongside his more engaging homilies. Around that time, he also let attendants of the Spanish-only mass that took place two hours earlier every Sunday to follow suit with their own much-needed spins.

That sort of inclusion was vital to the communities of these churches. Father Marty was one of the few Black priests I had ever come across, and the only American-born Black priest I knew of back then. No wonder he was looking for someone like me to join him. He needed a friend. Someone who understood the Black American experience. Someone who knew the electric slide was not the descriptor for a specific kind of damage caused by the storm surges of a major hurricane. Someone who could play a game of pitty-pat. (The Blacks collectively played spades, but this was the game I was used to kinfolk and friends playing at get-togethers.)

The "Come work for Jesus" moment took place during a routine confession. It was my first one since I had gone away for college, where, for the first time in my life, I stopped attending church regularly. A wave of guilt came over me because of this, so while on a holiday break I had hoped to share this fact with Father Marty, then say seven or twelve Hail Marys and feel better about myself.

Confessions were always tricky. Ideally, you'd sit there, air out *all* of your sins to the priest operating as God's customer-service rep, and then leave with a clean slate following those Hail Marys and Acts of Contrition. Unfortunately, the thing about Catholic guilt was that while it might have made you feel bad enough to want to go to confession, you might end up feeling too ashamed to actually confess all your sins. Typically, Catholics would confess their sins behind a wall, but at Saint Mark the Evangelist, you had to do a face-to-face—which made it even more difficult for me to open up. Normally, I would tell the priest a few things here and there, but never did I get blunt enough to blurt out something like, "Father Marty, I keep watching *Cruel Intentions* on tape and fast-forwarding to the part where Ryan Phillippe steps out of the pool butt-ass naked in order to masturbate."

Yeah, that wasn't happening.

What would often happen was that Father Marty would hear me air a few sins—like cursing—and then we'd segue into short conversations about our religion. Father Marty felt that, despite my age, I was pretty knowledgeable about Christianity. He was also well aware of my mother's commitment to the church and how those values were being instilled in her children. Given that she wanted grandchildren, I imagine she never had any intention of pushing me that far into the faith. After all, I was an altar boy only once, and the request happened at the very last minute during a Saturday mass (for those who cannot attend on Sunday, for reasons spanning from work to NFL games). But to an aging priest constantly pestering parishioners to pray for vocations to the priesthood, I looked like a top seed in the priestly draft.

Though at first I sat eye to eye in front of Father Marty and confessed the sins I didn't mind divulging, the small dimly lit beige room we were in began to feel smaller and darker as my confessional went on. I could tell in that moment that this wasn't going to be a routine confessional. The topic of which sins I may have committed shifted abruptly toward my take on those who committed their lives to God. I responded by saying individuals who chose to dedicate their lives to God ought to be commended for making the ultimate sacrifice. Translation: yes, it was very commendable and quite noble, but better them than me.

Evidently, my response further piqued his interest, and for a few moments he sat there in silence, seemingly pondering over what to say next. He began to stare at me in the midst of this silence. It was as if he were searching for something inside of me. Something that wouldn't lead to an investigation and a multimillion-dollar lawsuit and subsequent settlement later, mind you. He then questioned me about my age. I let him know that I was twenty, otherwise known as the best time to start engaging in the worst sins. He claimed that I appeared more mature than my age suggested. He added that he could feel a strong sense of spirituality in me. He noted that in these trying times, God needed the most capable of servants.

As we neared the end of my confessional, Father Marty looked at me and hit me with it: "I see a priest in you."

At that very moment, I felt my heart stop.

I'm sure Father Marty and me breaking into "Ave Maria" or the choreography from Kirk Franklin's "Stomp" might have been a more festive reaction, but I opted for muted shock and awe instead. Muted because I was at church and I couldn't yell, "You gotta be out of your rabid-ass mind, Father!" I guess hearing a religious person look at you and say you seem like a decent enough guy to serve God was quite the compliment. Yet all I did was question whether Father Marty suffered from cataracts or was starting to display early signs of dementia. How could he see a priest in me? Sure, I thought I knew a lot about Jesus and kept the recommended amount of Catholic guilt prescribed to parishioners. But me? A *priest*? At that period of my life, I saw my future self as something more along the lines of "Katie Couric with a dick." She had coanchors with penises, but as a longtime *Today* viewer, I preferred Katie over Bryant Gumbel, who seemed stiff and whose name select classmates would sometimes call me as a pejorative, and Matt Lauer, who often just came across as a dick. (Now, I had no idea he was *that* bad, per the accusations that led to his surprise ouster, but good fucking riddance all the same.) Katie was both serious and fun, and I saw myself being the same on the morning news one day. Father Marty was convinced otherwise, saying he felt strongly about his suspicions and advised me to give real consideration to ultimately joining the priesthood.

I was unsure as to whether he genuinely felt he saw a priest in me or he was he simply filling my head with thoughts of joining so that he could produce his yearly goal of one parishioner to the priesthood. His follow-up question made me wonder if I was special or if he merely said this to any male of applicable age: he asked me about college. I told him I was attending Howard University.

"You should pledge Omega Psi Phi. I will pay for it."

So not only did Father Marty see a priest in me but he also saw a fraternity guy. And not just any frat; he saw me as a Que Dog. In terms of Black fraternity and sorority stereotypes, I had been likened to an Alpha because they were smart or a Kappa because they were considered to be the pretty boys, but never a Que. Granted, I did have a habit of sticking out my tongue while dancing, but most wouldn't have pegged me as the type to be stepping to George Clinton's "Atomic Dog" and barking. (This is not an insult to them, 'cause there were quite a few Ques that were on Howard's campus that I would have taken down. But yeah, no. I'm not sure whether Father Marty was a Que, but he did often wear a purple priest's robe, which might have been a shout-out to that frat's colors?)

As I exited the confessional and proceeded to kneel before the pews to pray for forgiveness, I started to think of all the reasons I would not be right for the priesthood.

First, profanity and I had been in a committed relationship since childhood.

Second, while I had followed my mother's instructions to attend mass up until I went off to DC for school, no way could I attend seven times a week—much less perform it.

Third, I was not a fan of uniforms. I just couldn't see myself dolled up in one of those priestly dresses they were required to wear. I mean, I can appreciate how popes often dress like a bad bitch heading to an all-white party, but you know.

Reasons four through forever: I was a virgin and not keen on the idea of committing to a life of celibacy. You can't give up sex before experiencing it a couple dozen times. I've never understood the requirement that priests and nuns be celibate anyway. The rationale for it is well-known, but it doesn't make sense all the same: Jesus never talked much about sex, so why was sex sold to us as so impure and wrong outside of procreation? It was one of many questions I used to have in catechism, but rarely if ever were those questions answered with anything other than the sentiment that it was "God's way"—which was shorthand for "the hell if I know."

Father Marty was seeing me in ways I couldn't see myself. He believed in me, and even if it was confounding, it was flattering. As a result, it made me stop and reexamine the image I was projecting to others. I mean, several years prior to that day, I had looked at another priest during mass and daydreamed a bit about what it would be like to be him. (Note that around that same time, I contemplated a career as Batman too.) For a teensy bit after Father Marty's recruitment pitch, I felt like an ingrate for trying to think of reasons to deny what he had told me. I battled the question: "How dare you not at least consider it, after all your faith has done for you?" Catholic guilt never leaves you and follows you everywhere; it's the herpes of your conscience.

But the more I thought about it, the more I wondered if the religion I was so devoted to was more of a hindrance to my growth as a man than it was helpful. Much of my own dedication to my faith stemmed from fear of God's wrath in addition to the guilt and shame I suffered for harboring feelings that were in direct violation of God's will. I hadn't really challenged any of those beliefs until I was called upon to perpetuate them by joining the priesthood.

—

Once I went back to school, I began to seek information about God and sexuality beyond the prejudices I had been conditioned to accept. In time, I realized just how spiritually unaware I was. With a better understanding of the history and culture behind the words I used to cite for why I needed to never embrace or act upon my urges, I was reminded that the meanings of words could transform over time—even the word "abomination." And even if I were to disagree with that, technically all of the crawfish, shrimp, and crab I had been fed over the years made me just as hell-bound, if not more so, than the gay sex I wasn't having.

Then I reflected on my own immature ways of religion. Meanwhile, things never tempered down between my parents. My dad's anger and his troubling coping mechanisms never subsided, and I started to wonder increasingly whether religion kept my mom composed or captive. I admired her strength and faith tremendously, but I also speculated how much better her life might be if she focused more on what she could change now as opposed to waiting to be rewarded for her virtues in the afterlife. When you're suffering, faith can be an integral part of your survival. In my eyes, my mom was the strongest person in the world, and her religion had a lot to do with that. Even so, I didn't want to wait to die to live. I didn't want to keep bottling up who I was for the mere possibility that I might get a treat in the afterlife. Most of all, I never wanted to be in the position of causing some other person to feel as conflicted as I had been and continued to be.

I did not want to join the likes of Ted Haggard and Eddie Long, who were revealed to be harboring the very same-sex attractions that they consistently condemned from their pulpits. Had I actually listened to Father Marty, I might have gone on to face similar ordeals. Funnily enough, by the time Bishop Eddie Long was accused by former male congregants of sexual misconduct, I had an essay published in which I called upon Christians to consider placing homophobia among other biblically justifiable prejudices now deemed antiquated. Afterward, a college friend proceeded to email me what seemed like two years' worth of Bible study material. A year later, she found my new email address through my blog and wrote me again to say that she had met someone who prompted her to acknowledge that she liked women a whole lot more than she ever cared to admit. Despite the revelation, she closed her message with: "It's not something I broadcast. That's why I've always admired you. Being true to yourself is not easy."

It is not easy, and at the time I was approached to be a priest, it proved to be pivotal. I may not have seriously considered becoming one, but I was at a point in my life when I could have sunk myself into a system that didn't embrace me as warmly as I once embraced it. A form of religion that would tolerate me, but only the parts of me that weren't an affront to its misguided beliefs. The dangers in not using your God-given right of discernment were becoming painfully obvious. Although I was starting to open my mind and allow myself to see that not everything was as black and white as I assumed it to be, I wasn't exactly ready to let go of my religion completely or to publicly acknowledge my sexuality—but I *was* ready to figure some things out. Father Marty gave me the push I needed to finally start asking questions and finding answers, independently. I knew in my heart that God was not the cock-blocker so many would like us to believe. I just needed to go out and prove it.

The First, the Worst

I should have known it wouldn't end well, because our first date consisted of us seeing *Crash* and dining at a vegan restaurant. Although chicken is always the ideal option, the meatless food was good and far more satisfying than the film. As much as I loved Ryan Phillippe—his ass played a pivotal, defining role in my development—a film that examined racism and intolerance through narrative devices that recalled various after-school specials was not especially fulfilling to me. In my immediate feelings after leaving the theater, I found the film well-intentioned but okay at best. However, as time went on, the flaws about it became all the more apparent, and the experience of viewing it all the more regrettable.

The same could have been said about this dude.

We were at the Regal Cinema near Union Square. A rat ran up the theater steps at one point during the film. Of course, my clumsy ass dropped my phone in the dark as the movie played—technically, it was what I deserved for not having turned my phone off and opting to be present for the overpriced movie ticket I had purchased.

While he used the light from his phone to help me find mine, I desperately hoped that Master Splinter's ancestor wouldn't try to bite me and/or steal the phone. In hindsight, the rat was probably trying to communicate the warning *RUN, BITCH! RUN!* to me about this dude.

I first saw Jordan in passing while I was visiting with a high school friend who attended LIU Brooklyn. I was in New York to interview for an internship. I was a broadcast journalism major near the end of my sophomore year and was determined to get an internship in New York. I had already done a stint at Majic 102 in Houston and another at C-SPAN before that. But I needed an internship that could be directly applied to my major to get the credit I needed to graduate. However, by the time I started searching for one, it was starting to sink in that I was far too opinionated to play the role of traditional anchor. The veneer of objectivity in news was already fading, but not enough to convince me, the Black man with an increasingly slick mouth and strong point of view, that there was space for me. So while I thought someone needed to carry on the legacy of the late Ed Bradley and rock a single hoop earring on *60 Minutes*, I realized that I wasn't that person. Still, it was my major and I was not about to change it, which meant I needed to get it over with already, get my credit to graduate, and go about my business.

After the interview, I linked up with Lawrence, who had attended the same high school as me but was someone I knew more as the younger brother of a classmate. I was finally ready to flip my curiosity about sexuality into action, but I was still not officially out yet. I had heard about Lawrence being gay, so I decided to reach out.

I had wanted to go to New York City for multiple reasons. I, like many others before me, had dreamed of being in the city. I was a proud Howard University student, but my initial goal had been to attend NYU or Columbia. I wanted to be in NYC, not DC. I wanted to be free and successful, and New York represented the epitome of both to me. However, we didn't have enough money for Howard, much less NYU or Columbia, which cost more than twice as much. I eventually found my way to Howard because when I saw how many Black people I admired had matriculated there, I knew it wasn't a settlement of past dreams but a redirection into destiny.

Upon greeting Lawrence, it quickly dawned on me that he was no longer just somebody's little brother and very much a young man. He also made it clear that he was gay. Interestingly enough, we never discussed my sexuality directly, but based on how he spoke to me and discussed plans on where we would hang out that summer, he had already clocked me and possibly presumed that I would be far more forthcoming in due time. After hanging out in his dorms for about two hours, Lawrence walked me out so I could make my train in time.

That's when I spotted Jordan. If you ask me now who he looked like then, I would speedily say Bruno Mars. But Bruno Mars wasn't famous back then, so when I would describe him to friends at that time, I'd tell them he looked like a spare DeBarge. He spoke to Lawrence in passing while walking wherever he was going, and I got on the elevator and went back to DC. I couldn't shake his face out of my head, but fortunately, I had heard his first name.

It did not take long at all for me to comb Lawrence's Facebook friends and find him. Make note that this was Facebook in 2005. These young thots have no idea how good they have it now. Anyone can sign up for Facebook these days—including various democracy-soiling bots from a fake news factory based in Macedonia and founded by the Russians. Back then, you needed a college email address and the student-loan debt that came with it in order to sign up for the service.

I sent him a message that I had seen him. I mentioned how cute he was and that I was interested. He responded to my messages, but his responses were noticeably short. I was taking the hint, but decided to continue flirting for the sake of convincing myself that I was finally about this life and making real efforts to gain a footing in it. Not long after, Jordan shut me down by telling me that he was not gay. I gave myself credit for at least trying and then let it be. But days later, he circled back into my private messages, suddenly with an acknowledgment of having same-sex attractions and newfound interest in conversing with me. He said something about being private, and considering that I had hit him up out of the blue and only saw him in passing by way of a person who also lived in his dorm, he was somewhat suspicious.

Discretion was one thing, but secrecy was its own type of monster. For the sake of my own interest in him, I leaned in on the idea that he was being discreet rather than secretive. We continued talking on Facebook, then graduated to text, instant messenger, and occasional phone calls. He didn't give me a lot of information, but I thought he was cute. Damn cute. So cute that I decided to jump on a bus to go hang out with him in New York.

I took a bus from DC to see him in New York literally a day before I was to fly back to Houston for a week; after that, I would return to New York for my summer internship (not at *GMA*, oh well). I probably could have waited until I was actually living in New York for the summer, but I really wanted to see him, and, honestly, I wanted to finally go out with a boy. It was an impulsive move, but not the wrong one.

After we ate that vegan food, he took me to the Christopher Street Pier. Then we walked up Christopher Street a bit more until it was time for me to catch my bus, pack my stuff, and take myself to Houston before coming back to New York for the summer. As we were walking back up, two things happened that should have signaled to me that he was probably not going to be the person I imagined him to be—or someone I needed to be around. The first thing was some very assertive woman—clearly a native New Yorker—surveying us and saying, "Y'all look good together." I smiled, looked at him, and said, "I like her." As nervous as I was, I laughed a lot with him, and I smiled the entire time. I wasn't out yet and I wasn't sure what life as an admitted and eventually open gay man would look like, but in these moments, I felt the sort of assurance that I had been depriving myself of by not owning those feelings for so long. But then came the other thing: Jordan saw someone he knew and instantaneously became uneasy. As if he had something to hide. When I asked if there was a problem, he barely said anything about it. It was more like a gesture—a shrug—and it was not reassuring. I didn't have time to ask more because I needed to get back to DC.

—

During those summer months when I was in New York, it was difficult not only to get in touch with Jordan but also to physically see him. He worked a lot. He was also taking summer courses. He was "busy." Too busy for me, anyway. When I did see him in the flesh, I was reminded of why I liked him, but if someone is really into you, they behave differently, more enthusiastically. I did meet other dudes in the meantime. There was one in particular who had also gone to Howard. He wasn't my type, but he was handsome, smart, and, to some extent, amusing, in that he was trying to convey a certain hardness. It was the sort of abrasive, traditionally masculine posturing in which overcompensating Black men often engage. Given my background, that performative nonsense didn't draw much reaction beyond a chuckle. Like *Bless your heart, little boy, you ain't hard, and even if you were, I am no way shook.* But since we had gone to the same school, I was open to dating when we got back on campus.

He had different plans, however. The last time we hung out in New York, he informed me that he was not out on campus and had no intention of being so. He would not be dating men because he had other plans. Those other plans included pledging a fraternity and running for student government. He successfully did both, so I guess his plans worked out. As a consolation prize, he gave me head and threw that big, country booty in the air. I let him blow me, but I did not go all the way with him. That was for a few reasons. First, I was a virgin, so in that moment, he was the first person to suck my dick. (For that, I am forever grateful.) Having said that, I operated under the belief that the first time I had sex would be with someone I cared about. Someone who would make an awkward experience on which I had no insight more comfortable to engage in. So, while I liked this dude, I liked Jordan far more.

I kept in touch with Jordan when I went back to Howard. By early fall, I was back on his campus, albeit to stay with Lawrence and hang out some more with the people I had met through him. When I went down to their cafeteria for breakfast, I saw Jordan. He spoke to me but was noticeably distant. I saw why: He had some kind of girlfriend. Claudia was introduced to me briefly by way of Lawrence. She was pretty, seemed really nice, and was Latina—

which I would later learn was kind of a thing for Jordan. Jordan was a fake-ass Latino in that he was very much some country Black boy from Long Beach but had curly hair that kind of made him look ambiguous to people who didn't know the various ways in which Black people can present. Even I wasn't all that familiar with these subtleties, so I recall asking, "Ain't your ass just Black?" He was, but evidently he had a preference.

I should have immediately written Jordan off after this, but I listened to his rationale. It was the kind that a no-good man in a Black nineties romantic comedy gave. *Yeah, she likes me, and we've hung out, but that's not a thing.* She thought differently, of course. To the point that a few weeks later, I got a phone call from her asking if Jordan and I had some kind of thing. Who had said something to her? I assumed it had been one of Lawrence's gossipy friends. I never did get a definitive answer, but I covered for Jordan all the same. For someone who felt scarred by all the stereotypical images of gay Black men that I saw in media, it was rather ironic and ridiculous for me to be willing participant in a collegiate version of that god-awful "down-low brother" hysteria. But I wanted Jordan to like me. I wanted him to like me too much—till it came at the expense of my own integrity.

Still operating from the house of idiocy, I invited Jordan to come down to DC for Howard's homecoming. I had a plan in mind: I would rent a car and a hotel, we would hang out, party, get drunk, and then have sex. I knew he was far more experienced sexually than I was, so I was willing to let him, uh, lead, and formally introduce me to homosexuality. I had a sneaking suspicion based on my porn searches which side of sex felt more natural, but I thought, *I am falling in love with this person, and with love, I will probably like it from him.* This was what happened when you listened to too many Mariah Carey ballads.

By the time he got to DC, I was under so much stress. I had experienced bad luck in landing in some of the classes I needed to finish my major, so I was taking twenty-one credits in order to graduate on time. I was also the president of the student chapter of the National Association of Black Journalists, a position I had never wanted but had been pressured into taking because I was the most experienced person left in the organization. On top of that, I was a staff writer for the student newspaper, the *Hilltop*. As a result of doing too much, I rarely slept, had constant headaches, and was setting myself up for a fight with my body that I would undoubtedly lose. On the first night of our hotel stay, Jordan found me passed out in the bathroom. I had absolutely no idea what had happened. I ended up blacking out again two months later at home, where I knocked my head on something (A cabinet? A sink? I don't know, I blacked out) and had to be taken to the emergency room because I was dizzy, couldn't see anything, and could barely talk. A CAT scan found nothing wrong, but I was told that my stress levels were extremely high and that I needed to cut back. The end result was me failing a math class and staying an extra semester that eventually became an extra year. The additional debt was far from appreciated (though at least I wasn't dead).

On the next night of homecoming, we went to a club called Love. We had the best time—until it ended with us both being robbed at gunpoint. You see, before DC became gentrified beyond recognition, Love was located in an area—Northeast DC—that wasn't especially nice. I had wanted to go ahead and pay to park in a lot, but Jordan said no, we could just park on the street. As someone from "the hood," I was wary of this, but didn't want to argue about it. However, when he told me where to park, I did note that it didn't look like the safest place.

"It's fine."

So fine that after leaving the club and going to our cars, I turned around to see a gun in Jordan's face; another man put one in mine. My initial thought was "Fuck, I am a terrible date." I had gone from blacking out one night to a jacking the next. None of this was that sexy shit. Jordan was used to being robbed, though, as I later found out. I suppose they thought he looked like a member of B2K and was easy to rob. *Okay, but don't drag me down with you.* I gave them my wallet but kept my phone and the rental car keys. But they got everything Jordan had.

When we got back to the hotel, I called my mom to tell her to cancel my credit cards. Hours later, she called me to say she was surprised at how calm I had sounded. I told her, "That's 'cause I won all these scholarships and took out all these loans to go here, and I coulda got robbed at home for free." As for the police officer, a Black woman with a hairstyle that felt a decade too old but woulda been cute for Halle Berry in *Boomerang,* she spent much of the time bemoaning how much she couldn't stand Howard and a lot of Howard students. *I just got jacked at gunpoint, and you want to bitch to me about my Bison brethren? Girl, give me this lil' piece of paper just in case I need to send it to my bank or credit card companies and fuck off forever.*

The next morning, Jordan and I woke up around the same time, and I had an idea: teach me how to suck dick. He laughed at my phrasing, but while the act doesn't necessarily require instructions, he coached me anyway. I wanted to do more, but he said no.

I wanted to have sex, but he declined. I was both offended and embarrassed. We went to the homecoming game after that. My friend Sarah, whom I will love forever, slid me $50 to get me through the rest of the weekend, and after the game let out, I took Jordan to the bus station and he went back to New York.

Literally days after that, he fessed up: that he was seeing someone else—not a woman this time—and that they were now official. I wanted to scream, *Why in the fuck did you come here, then? You dumb-ass bitch!* but instead I just sighed a whole lot and tried to get myself off the phone. That should have been the end of him, but it wasn't. We still talked every so often. I still flirted with him, and sometimes he would flirt back. I still wanted to have sex with him.

Several months went by, and I was back in New York for another summer of interning: Chris Rock had a comedy-writing program with Comedy Central, and I was one of the lucky eight participants. I saw Jordan the morning I moved into the NYU dorm the network put us up in. He wasn't with that boy anymore, but as I later learned, he'd carried on with the same bullshit. With him, it was a lot of interest expressed whenever I wasn't in his physical presence. When I was, he would hold back or be completely disengaged. One of the few times we hung out around that time, he introduced me to one of his closest friends. I had met some of his friends before, but not any from back home. We went to karaoke, and they were surprised I had never done karaoke before. I hadn't because I hated the idea of karaoke, and after doing a rendition of the Isley Brothers' "Between the Sheets" and Slim Thug's verse on Beyoncé's "Check on It," I confirmed my disdain for it. Jordan took my karaoke virginity, and all I got in the end was another instance of gross disrespect.

After a while, some Latino boy showed up, and you had to have been a blind moron not to notice that this boy was into Jordan.

"You wouldn't bring someone else you're talking to around me, would you?" I asked. Jordan said no, but then I saw them holding hands at one point. I wanted to grab my glass of cheap well brown liquor, gulp it down, and then crack that glass over his head. Instead of catching a case, I left abruptly. Before all this happened, I lent him a shirt to wear on his job interview. When he invited me to come get it back, I could make out the boy in the background, in Jordan's bed. I told him he was a dishonest piece of shit, grabbed my shirt, and left.

We didn't speak much after that. I went back to school. Although the extra year made me feel like I had failed a bit, at least I was able to graduate in a year that Oprah Winfrey was the commencement speaker. No, I didn't like her down-low-themed conspiracy peddling, but it was Oprah. I loved Oprah. I could feel my credit score rising as she inspired us to go off into the world and let our purposes guide us. She told us not to worry; that we were in good hands because God had our back. That "Howard teaches you to define yourself by your own terms and not by somebody else's definition." That there was no such thing as failure because failure was merely "God's way of pointing you in a new direction."

I applied this advice toward the future that awaited me in my professional life, but it was also something I wished to apply to my personal life. Jordan had left me feeling like a failure. I had accepted myself for my sexuality, but I wanted someone I found attractive to find me desirable in turn. I wanted an ideal setting to let go of my inhibitions and experience my sexuality in totality. I wanted to connect with someone emotionally before I connected with them physically. I wanted it my way. None of this was wrong, per se, but my mistake was that I had been pursuing a man who had never been the person I had pretended he was. We had enjoyed moments in which we opened up with each other. When I told him about my chaotic childhood, he told me about his own issues with his father. When I told him that I wanted to be a successful writer who would go on to do all of these amazing things, he let me in on his dream of being a singer. I encouraged his dreams the way he encouraged mine. But I also worked harder on achieving mine. I had plenty of insecurities, but I didn't have as many as he did—particularly about being a gay man. If I was on the road to acceptance of self, I should not have been so eager to race after a man who was traveling in a completely different direction than I was. I was the only one trying to make something really happen, and I did this despite sign after sign telling me to let it go. I didn't feel like a failure for trying, but I did regret my reaction to what I perceived to be a failure.

—

When I finally lost my virginity, it was to one of his friends. It was not the sort of gotcha that some people do in order to get back at a person they feel wronged them. What happened was, I was back in New York job hunting, and while out with Maiya, with whom I was staying, we went to a gay club. Given that Maiya was one of the first people I told that I was gay, she wanted me to be in a space made for me. We drank, we danced, we drank even more as we continued to dance. Then I ran into Adam, one of Jordan's friends, and he joined us until Mai decided to dip. "Keep partying" is what she said.

I asked about Jordan and how he was doing. Adam told me he was fine, but then, nearly out of the blue, Adam told me that he had sex with Jordan and was very descriptive about everything they had done together. It infuriated me. I kept drinking. I didn't need to be drinking anymore, as I was already drunk enough, but I had been given information that I wished I had never known.

I don't remember everything that happened next, but I do remember the key points. I recall knocking out a bit on the couch at the club and Adam helping me get up while letting his hands linger in places they shouldn't have. Before we left, I asked for water. I don't remember drinking the water. All I remember is we were walking in some residential area nowhere near where I needed to be and Adam was moving in to kiss me. I didn't push him off, but he had more in mind than just making out. A lot of the homes in New York have basements, so they also have steps that lead to that downstairs area. He took me into one such place, pulled down my pants, and repeated some of the very acts he had described doing to Jordan. I didn't want this, but I didn't stop him. He pulled my pants down farther, lowered me down, and quite quickly put himself in me. And with that, he took my virginity.

I don't remember how I got home, but I remember feeling disgusted with myself. I hadn't enjoyed myself physically or in any other way imaginable. This was not how I wanted to lose my virginity. This was not the person to whom I wanted to lose my virginity. Hell, that wasn't even the position I wanted to be in sexually to lose my virginity. I wanted to be the one in *control*, and this was *thriller*! None of this was what I wanted. And yet, I had let it happen. I had let it happen because I got drunk and drunker in reaction to information that, when it boiled down, had hurt my feelings. I am not excusing him for taking advantage of me. I am just disappointed in myself for never wanting to engage in that type of risky behavior only to do just that while inebriated and emotionally wounded.

I told Jordan about it much, much later. He was bothered that Adam had told me their business and was apologetic because he knew that I wanted sex to be special. It may not have been his fault, but I resented him for everything else. He knew as much, and whenever we did speak, it would always go back to how I had been wronged. I said I had forgiven him, but I hadn't. He was still upset with me over some things I had told him in the heat of the moment. It didn't matter, though. We were not near each other, and it felt right to just go about our lives. I had no expectations of ever seeing him again. And that was fine.

Unfortunately, because God loves to troll, I ended up being in the same metropolitan area as Jordan a couple of years later. For me, I was dream-chasing in Los Angeles, and for him, he was back home in Long Beach doing . . . the hell if I know. I learned this because of Facebook, where I should have had him blocked. But I can be so hardheaded sometimes. I reached out to him, and while texting back and forth, we decided that maybe we should hang out under the pretense that what had happened was in the past and we could just move forward. He did seem different in the ways in which he talked about himself and where he felt he was going. He was different in how he talked to me as well. Even when annoyed out of my mind with him, I had a habit of still being flirtatious.

He proposed a plan: that we do what we hadn't done years ago in that hotel room. I professed a bit of shock that he would say this, but I let him know that it was fine with me. So we kept talking about it, which caused me to believe that while we may never be a couple, we could act like one. In the past, I had always called him my fake boyfriend because he gave me the kind of grief you have with a trifling partner but none of the perks. But now, the perks appeared to finally be on the horizon.

It never happened. The day we were supposed to link, something came up. Something *kept* coming up. Then he fizzled away. He hadn't changed. Jordan was the same person with seemingly good intentions who turned out to be a self-centered jackass. The sort of person who would lead people on because they enjoyed the way someone made them feel. I conflated his ego with his having real feelings for me. I hated how he made me feel. I hated that he played me. I hated that in allowing him to play me, I played the hell out of myself. I hated that he only bolstered so many lingering insecurities in me. My talking to him, albeit infrequently, was my way of keeping the lines of communication open with the underlying hope that one day, we could have that moment. But I was seeking validation from the wrong source. I kept trying to repress my anger at him by forcing civility with the hopes that he would give me something I wanted. Something I felt would help an awkward, humiliating situation make more sense. The mistake was to see it all for what it was: I had tried, and it hadn't worked out. I had tried way too hard and for too long when I should have let it go.

All the same, I may have failed in losing my virginity in the way I envisioned, and I may not have gotten Jordan to want me as much as I wanted him, but I did learn from the experience. I couldn't make someone love me. I couldn't make myself desirable to someone who didn't want me. I couldn't compel someone to see me in the way in which I wanted to be seen. All I could do was be myself, and if someone didn't fool with it, find someone else. I didn't quite master that with dudes that came after Jordan, but with him, I reached a place where I could let him go.

—

By dumb luck, I saw him again years after the exchange that had led to nothing. I had finally moved to New York as an adult, rather than merely spending time there for a summer to intern or as some frequent visitor. I was standing in line for a concert when I saw him walk toward the end of it. Our eyes met around the same time, and we both spoke. By then, I no longer carried that same degree of hostility. He apologized many times for things that he'd done and said, but mostly for how he had made me feel. I had heard some of these same apologies in the past, but I hadn't thought he truly meant them. By then, though, I decided to stop giving so much energy to him and what did and did not happen with us.

I let him wait in line with me and the friend with whom I had come to the show. He let me know that his boyfriend would eventually be joining him. He wanted to let me know that he had someone. Maybe he had a flashback to past acts of foolishness that woulda got him popped. Whatever the reason, gold star for him having a man, but that didn't matter anymore to me. His appearance had changed, but he remained cute enough for at least a (hate) fuck.

I snapped out of it. Once we both got into the venue and the concert started, Jordan and his boyfriend stood near us, but I didn't look their way. I wanted to enjoy the show in front of me rather than fixate, yet again, on a distraction.

Diana Ross

I didn't know there was a National Coming Out Day until my late twenties. This makes sense, given that the holiday had been conceived the decade I was born. It also doesn't help that I wasn't brought up in an environment that would welcome such celebrations. The same can be said of society at large. After all, the first president I actually paid attention to was Bill Clinton, the architect of "Don't ask, don't tell." We now live in an age in which social media magnifies the most trivial of celebrations, such as National Pancake Day or National Chicken Wing Day (to be fair, chicken wings are one of the greatest gifts to the modern carnivore), so thankfully, in the midst of learning about celebrations like National Jalapeño Popper Day and You Can Remember Buying Cassette Maxi-Singles Day, I also learn about days like National Coming Out Day. Perhaps this is how a lot of folks feel about Juneteenth, which I learned was not as commonly known outside of Texas as I thought. However, no one challenges that day after learning about it, yet every single October 11, some bemoan the necessity of the occasion in the first place. The critics all use different phrasing to plead their case, but their arguments are all roughly the same:

Why does anyone need to come out? Straight people don't come out, so why should anyone else? Why is it anyone's business, anyway? Doesn't National Coming Out Day help perpetuate the notion that heterosexuality is the norm? Aren't members of the LGBTQ*SWV* community much safer now than in the past?

It's the most annoying pop quiz ever.

Nonstraight people come out because the world continues to render everyone straight until otherwise noted. Straight people don't have to come out because there are more of them than there are of us. It's not anyone's business, and no one is obligated to hold a press conference to reveal their sexual orientation, but in terms of visibility and raising awareness on a human level, "coming out" continues to matter. As for being safer, that depends on who you are and where you are. Even in this country, which, with the assistance of voter suppression, sexism, racism, xenophobia, a hostile foreign government, and a complicit for-profit media, elected a bigot—a bigot who, in the past, may not have been overtly homophobic or transphobic, but like the opportunistic, careless person that he is, quickly sacrificed our safety and our basic human rights for his political interests.

I largely hear complaints about National Coming Out Day only from those who may not necessarily be in the closet but who nevertheless don't overtly profess their sexuality for careerist reasons. That, or they're people who see society through the lens of an early-1990s Mariah Carey ballad rather than seeing the horror flick directly in front of them. So, yes, National Coming Out Day continues to matter. The day Diana Ross's "I'm Coming Out" stops slapping at a gay bar is the day we can band together and put National Coming Out Day in rice—not a second sooner.

I myself came out in stages.

By the time I had settled in New York to intern for the summer, I went ahead and told Lawrence directly what I had only alluded to mere months beforehand. Not long after that confession, Lawrence took me to my first gay club—Luke & Leroy's in the West Village.

Back in high school, quite a few of my friends—mostly lesbians or bisexual girls—used to go to this club in Houston called Big Yo's! The club used to advertise on television specifically during BET's *Uncut*—which played music videos that in no way could air during daytime or even prime time, like Black Jesus's "What That Thang Smell Like"—or on the local public-access station, which played all the Southern rap videos that were not getting national airplay. The club was technically eighteen and up, but like many gay clubs of yore, if you had a fake ID, knew how to present older, or, frankly, the person at the door didn't give that great a fuck, you could routinely get in. I never went, though. My mom was strict and enforced an oppressive curfew. As for sneaking out, well, we had burglar bars on the door, so it wasn't exactly easy to do. (My brother sure tried, and he got popped in the mouth a few times as a consequence.)

So, having absolutely no experience in a gay club before this night out with Lawrence, I immediately expressed confusion to him over the scene before me: two hurly-burly dudes dancing in the dark with each other. To which Lawrence replied, "Fool, we're in a gay club." And we would go to this club every Thursday night, me stupidly using the credit card I had no business owning in order to drink excessive amounts of alcohol. Part of this was to loosen me up, but much of it was rooted in my attraction to Chris the Bartender. Chris the Bartender went to Princeton, where he majored in mechanical engineering. I knew this because when I wasn't dancing excessively to Destiny's Child's "Lose My Breath," to nearly every song in Lil' Kim's catalog, and thankfully, to selections from the snap music era, I was talking to Chris the Bartender. Chris the Bartender told me he was straight, but he thought I was funny and I thought he should have my babies, so I kept talking to him. I also tipped well, which explains why he both engaged with me and sometimes gave me extra alcohol or free shots. I convinced myself that he loved me but that he was afraid of commitment. Once, I left the club for a second and returned with a Ring Pop to propose to him. He was flattered, but I am not married. We became Facebook friends, if that's anything.

As all this was going on, I completely avoided all my friends from Howard. Most of them were women. I imagine they had their suspicions about me, given that I had never tried to smash any of them and the only woman I talked about with enthusiasm was named Beyoncé. Still, I didn't feel ready to confirm their suspicions. That all changed, however, after the way I carried myself during Pride events that same summer. I initially had an aversion to going and was practically coerced into doing so. I was so petrified of being found out—and lo and behold, it happened within minutes of my being there. There were so many different folks from so many separate parts of my life—more people from high school, people from college, people from the Taylor Michaels Scholarship program, founded by Magic Johnson, for which we were flown out from separate cities across the country and housed together for a week—and all of them randomly popped up on me, one after the other.

I remember being at the Christopher Street Pier laughing and smoking a Black & Mild with Lawrence and his friends when I saw a bunch of folks from our high school heading our way. I immediately took off. I had always regretted not running track in high school, and the speed with which I sprinted away yielded another reason why. I knew that if they saw me, they would report me to people back home, and it would get back to my brother, who I had heard was gay too. Despite our closeness in age, we were not especially close at the time, so I didn't bother inquiring further about him and I didn't want him to know anything about me either. It may have been my own paranoia, but I feared that he would run off and tell my folks.

After escaping, I ran into the girl from the scholarship program who, almost immediately upon meeting me two years prior, had kept making pointed remarks about my sexuality. She was sitting on a step on Christopher Street. She used to whisper behind my back to our shared group of friends in the program. Some defended me, some didn't; most didn't care either way. The irony was that, as much as she worried about me, I had a sneaking suspicion that she was gay too. I suppose fixating on me was a solid way to deflect from her own struggle with accepting her sexual identity.

Yet here she was, standing before me with a smug grin on her face. Initially I thought to speed by, but after quickly turning my back to her, I stopped in my tracks. It was then that I asked myself what exactly I was running from. Better yet, was I really about to let this messy motherfucker have one over on me? For as much shame as I still carried with me, I did not like other people thinking they had something on me. I'd known I liked boys since being caught at daycare trying to get this boy to show me his lil' cupcakes. Of all people to hide from, it was not going to be her.

Now, here on Christopher Street, I walked up to her directly.

"Hi. Now you have it confirmed."

She feigned shock and reached for a hug. I gave her fake ass the fake-ass church hug she deserved. Then I went back to the pier to apologize for scattering away like a damn fool. While walking back, I spotted someone I knew from Howard. I walked up to him with a smile on my face.

"Hey. Don't you go to Howard?"

He ran from me as I had run away from others minutes prior. It hurt, but I understood it. I had almost done the same thing back-to-back.

—

While I was interning at MTV, there was a girl there named Brooke who worked as the executive assistant for the president of MTV News. The day I started that internship, I got on the wrong Q train and headed to Brooklyn rather than 1515 Broadway. I still managed to make it to work on time, but the head of the news division sat me down and said, "Give me a few minutes. I'm going to get you settled." He never did. I had to find my own work, so I walked around the office and constantly asked people what they did and how I could be of use. While doing my routine tours, I finally talked to Brooke; from then on, I was constantly walking by her desk. I didn't know what it was about her, but I felt more comfortable with her than I did some of my actual friends. During one of our chats, she randomly inserted that I should "just be free." Usually, I would dismiss that as some hippy jargon to which my cynical ass couldn't relate. However, in that moment, I just smiled. The woman had a point, and the more I thought about that nugget of advice, the more eager I became to apply it.

That led to my finally deciding to tell one person from Howard about my sexuality: Maiya.

I asked Mai if she wanted to go to lunch, and we went to Sylvia's in Harlem. (It's still the only time I've ever eaten at Sylvia's, despite the fact that I've lived by it for years.) There, over catfish and macaroni and cheese, I stumbled over something I had fought to say out loud for all of my life.

"I'm gay."

"Oh, I knew that. My mom is a psychiatrist."

Girl, that is not the response you're supposed to give! Now, I imagine what truly tipped her off (you know, besides whatever mannerisms she deemed obvious: obsessing over the first half of *Dangerously in Love*; not hearing anything about my dick in some Howard girl's vagina) was when I once heard a very loud display of homophobia in class and promptly raised my hand to shut the dumb shit the fuck down.

Right at the start of the fall semester, I told a second person from Howard—Nakisha, another I forever will adore. We were in the iLab and she wanted to know why we didn't hang out. After I told her, she playfully slapped my face and said, "Duh! Why didn't you tell me? We could've went to the gay clubs together!" I love my friend dearly, but for future reference, "DUH" is not the preferred response. You don't have to feign shock (although sometimes a little theatrics helps), but generally speaking, you never know what anyone is until they tell you explicitly. Even if Kish had seen me doing the Bunny Hop (a dance, non-southerners) on the rainbow flag while juggling dicks, as a courtesy, I would prefer to be given the benefit of the doubt. Then again, she is from The Bay and has fully functional eyes. There's only so much I can ask of a good friend.

After a while, Lawrence went back to Houston for a break, and I was going to Luke & Leroy's, as well as other gay clubs in the area, solo dolo. In hindsight, I should have brought Nakisha, as she was bait for gay men.

I got more surprising remarks from other classmates—one of whom expressed immediate disappointment because she thought I was cute. A few more echoed that sentiment, but I was like, "Uh, when I tried girls, y'all didn't want me, so let me just go work through this boy thing I've been bottling down since *Chip 'n Dale: Rescue Rangers*." My coming out became more real when I told my best friend back home.

"Kimmie, I'm gay."

Kim expressed legitimate shock, but, as expected, delivered a sharp, memorable response.

"It was that bitch Alicia, wasn't it?"

I had to explain to Kim that while it did feel like Alicia *had* run over my heart with her Dodge Neon, that was not how it worked. After that, she just accepted it, as did the other friends from high school with whom I maintained contact. I told my friends first because they were my chosen family. That's not to say that I didn't love my family, but I had also gone far away from Houston for college for multiple reasons—though one large motivating factor was escaping what had always felt like an environment mired in chaos.

My brother did hear about me and called me about it. At first, I told him to mind his own fucking business and that he didn't know what in the fuck he was talking about. Knowing that response was mean as hell and totally unwarranted, I called him back, apologized, and explained the truth calmly (I do not like to be met with gossip, much less from my own brother).

The family member whose opinion mattered most to me was

my sister, Nicole. I was, and am, obsessed with my sister. Growing up, she was nine years older than I was, but because our mom often worked long hours overnight or twelve-hour day shifts, my sister had a large hand in taking care of us.

I can barely put into words how much I fell before the altar of my big sister. My appreciation for music came largely from diving into her massive CD collection. My appearance grew majorly from her helping me shop. My parents were incredibly hard workers, but the way my sister managed to get pregnant at twenty-two with my oldest niece, continue to have both a full-time job and a full course load, and still graduate with good grades inspired me beyond belief. How she continued to work tirelessly as others failed in their responsibilities left me in awe. And she cared so much for her children and worked relentlessly not to repeat any of our parents' mistakes. We were both so hard on ourselves, but she was nothing short of impeccable, so if she had not accepted my being gay, it would have broken me.

I didn't tell her until a year after I told my friends and my brother.

I was back in New York on a random trip to see Jordan. At some bar, drunk and tired, I let the liquid courage direct me to call my sister out of the blue to tell her the complete truth about me. Sensing my anxiety, she said, "Uh, okay. I mean, I kind of wondered at one point, but I wasn't totally sure. Are you all right?" I wasn't sure if she was in total acceptance in that moment, but the fact that her main concern was whether or not I was okay was another reason why I love her so much. Today, I still talk to her more than any other member of my family.

—

My parents were another story.

My friends were top priority. My sister was next. My parents . . . always knew that conversation would be difficult. So I waited. And waited. Then waited some more. A few years went by before any discussions were had about it, and each time, I felt that the chats stemmed from coercion.

As for my father, he asked me about my sexuality in a way that would have been unsurprising to anyone who had ever met him. He pulled me to the side in the living room of the house in which I had grown up and asked me if I was "funny." When he uttered the word "funny," his left hand moved swiftly side to side. This country-ass way of describing homosexuality immediately turned me off. My first instinct was to repeat the hand gesture and declare, "I'm hilarious." But I did something else instead: I didn't confirm or deny. This was not about denying who I was; it was about punishing a man who I felt had made all our lives a living hell. Of course, remembering how he talked about his own brother, I was not sure how he would handle the news, but I did have my suspicions.

He will blame my mother.

He will get angry.

He will say something hurtful.

He will piss me the fuck off.

We might likely fight.

As an adult, I had to be separated from him once after calling him a bitch to his face over the way he spoke to my mother. Between his volatility and my repressed anger issues—ones shaped squarely by him—that would have ended very badly. The same can be said for this line of questioning.

Even so, none of this was my ultimate concern or why I didn't say anything one way or the other. I knew he knew. He knew that I knew that he knew. I just looked at him with utter disdain for asking me because I knew it would hurt him. All I said was "I don't like anything," and added that no matter if I was the gayest or the straightest man within a twenty-mile radius, I didn't owe anyone an explanation and that I would tell my mother anything before I told him. He would complain that my sister and I "hated him" and that we only talked to our mother. Never did he make note that his actions may have led to such allegiances.

I let years go by before telling my mom. What prompted my doing so was the publication of an essay that I had written about two young boys who reportedly committed suicide within the same month after being bullied for being gay. This was before the "It Gets Better" movement. These were two young Black boys, and the world wasn't often as responsive to their needs as it was to those of white kids. For *The Root*, I wrote about my own history of taunts over being gay and how I wish I could have told each bullied boy that he would overcome these challenges. Back then, *The Root* had a relationship with MSN, and some of my pieces would be picked up on their homepage—sometimes only for a few hours. But in the case of this essay, it was up for much of the whole day, and squarely in the center of the homepage. MSN's site used to be my mom's homepage. I wasn't certain, but I had a strong belief that it was likely she would see the piece, read it, and be disgusted. Such reasoning was why the piece almost hadn't happened, in fact. My editor had me speak to a colleague at the site—another gay Black man—to gauge whether

or not I was ready for the potential consequences of publicly out-
ing myself in my work. By the time he called me, my decision was
already made—and he picked up on that quickly.

The piece went live. I called my mom. Her reaction was one I
will never forget. One I wrestle with forgiving her for.

"So what are you trying to say to me? That you're gay."

"Yes."

"Well, that explains why you and your brother's lives have gone
the way they have."

Of all the hurtful things she's said to me—that I was a "self-
centered bastard" for wanting to go away for college knowing we
didn't have the money (she apologized after I confronted her about it
later) or that I would end up alone—this was the most hurtful. I also
didn't know what in the hell she was talking about. Was I rich? No,
but by twenty-five, after the Great Recession and media imploding as
the shift to digital occurred, I was managing to support myself with
my words. I had made an appearance on national TV for my work
and was continuing to build my career. I was not without struggle,
thanks to my oppressive private student loan debt, but those struggles did not mirror my brother's. Not to mention, those struggles had
absolutely nothing to do with sexuality. If anything, many of them
were influenced by the man she had decided to keep lying with, not
the other way around. She had her fucking nerve to say otherwise.

My mama went on to express disappointment about likely not
having grandchildren anymore. I noted that technology could fix
this, but she promptly dismissed it. After that phone call ended,
I didn't speak to her for months. I imagine she worried about my
health. I'm sure she felt that as a Black man in this world, I had
enough problems. Why further complicate them? I wish she had

said that while she didn't agree with my "lifestyle choices," she at least hoped that I would be safe. I wish she had said anything besides what she had actually said.

She was cold, mean, and condescending. I wanted to curse her out, outline detail by detail how she was nowhere near the sort of Christian she thought she was, and tell her to never talk to me again. I'm glad I didn't stoop to her level in that moment—as much as I wanted to. By the time we spoke again, neither of us brought up what had been previously discussed.

A few years later, someone asked me if I could choose to be straight, would I? I thought about it for a second and started to lean toward one answer, but then looked up and saw a man walking down the street in basketball shorts and an undershirt that I still need to quit calling a "wife beater." He had a Caesar, his sleeve was tatted, and he was just the right level of shortness I tend to go for. In full-fledged creep mode, I told my friend to hold for a second so I could watch him. As soon I looked down at his ass, I quickly turned around and said, "Nah, I'm good with gay."

But I never forgot the hurt I felt by my mother's words. It further strained an already-strained familial dynamic and had an impact on me in ways I wouldn't realize until much, much later in my adulthood. As a gay man, you already have so many people against you. Your family—especially your mother—is supposed to be in your corner as you battle these people, not throwing sucker punches along with them. As hurt as I was, it did not stop me from becoming more personal in my work. If anything, it lit a fire under me to advocate even more for those like me. Those who faced similar struggles. Those who worried that their mother, the most important person in their lives, would be disappointed by something that's beyond our control.

Folks can feign that the world is much more progressive than it is, but my story still mirrors that of far too many others. Thus, there is the need to continue sharing it and to push the same acceptance of others. Not everyone else has to do this, but for those of us who do, we know why we have to. We are worthy of acceptance, but far too many continue to not view us or treat us as such—notably those with power. We can't shut up until they do.

You Will Die Poor

t was becoming painfully apparent to me that I needed to get out of Houston—the sooner, the better. It was fall 2008, and I was full of frustration and feeling like the biggest fucking failure. I graduated from Howard a year later than I was supposed to. (Pro tip: try not to overexert yourself by cramming twenty-one credits a semester into your senior year in addition to holding a staff-writer job on the school paper, being president of the student chapter of the National Association of Black Journalists, taking algebra at the very last minute knowing damn well that mathematics is the archvillain of your life as a student, and having the nerve to start blacking out and having a bunch of weird health problems. It won't end well for you.) I didn't get a job immediately after college. Well, I did eventually get a job offer to work with one of my favorite people in media ever, Danyel Smith, as her assistant; only when she told me she might be leaving her position at *Vibe* two months after my start date, I punked out. I got a letter saying I would be owing about $800 a month in private student-loan payments, and after comparing that with the offered salary, I took the advice of my family members who don't work in media and declined the offer after accepting it, annoyed Danyel (we're better now, I love her), and ended up living at home for a year and a half trying to fight off their suggestions I go do something else like teach or anything else besides media. I was scrabbling freelance jobs together and constantly hounding people's inboxes searching for an in—a job, a writing contract, a referral, whatever would help advance my goals—but after more than a year back home, I was feeling lost.

I needed to be someplace where I could realistically pursue my dreams. If I waited too much longer, I was going to need to get fitted for a straitjacket. Such fears led to me reluctantly taking Lauren's offer to rent a room in her four-bedroom apartment in Los Angeles.

Shortly before leaving, my uncle Terry stopped by to give me some advice and to confirm that I was making the right decision to stop bullshitting and leave Houston again. I hadn't seen that much of Uncle Terry as I grew older. Indeed, I didn't see much of my dad's family at all, sans a few relatives every few years. But Terry always made his presence felt somehow.

I was in bed, recovering from the previous night of cathartic debauchery, when I heard him—his voice, loud as all hell—talking to my brother Marcus. At the time, my brother worked for the county, and that got Terry excited. He made the following declaration: "Man, the next time they take me downtown, I'm going to say, 'My nephew works upstairs, let me out this motherfucker!'" He was always a man with a plan, but a loud plan that woke me up. He asked Marcus where I was, and Marcus told him that I was asleep. "Shit, I'm about to wake his ass up." *Too late for that, Uncle Terry.*

I wanted to fake being asleep or play dead, but I knew that he was usually fresh out of damns and was unlikely to spare one in this instance. The light was turned on as I heard Terry shout, "Nigga, wake yo' ass up!"

I didn't recognize him (in this moment he looked a lot like Rick James). However, he remained very much the same Uncle Terry who, as legend has it, once introduced a former in-law to one of his girlfriends as "the bitch that broke up my brother's marriage." The same Uncle Terry, who, after finding out that I had graduated from Howard University and was trying to launch a career as a writer, asked, "When you gon' work in a building?" Shortly thereafter, he asked me to burn him a couple of movies for him on DVD. He looked like he was about to sing "Mary Jane" at any moment, but it was the same hysterical, slick-mouthed Uncle Terry (still committed to looking like Rick James).

"What you doing still asleep? You must have been partying all last night."

I answered "Maybe," only to add, "I probably got that from you." Uncle Terry laughed. He took my smart-ass response as a compliment to his own smart-ass comment—the family way. He told me my dad had mentioned something about LA and asked what had happened to my plans about moving to New York. I explained that I thought California might be the better option for me for the time being, and his face lit up as if I had pulled out a blunt. He then told me that LA was "fast" and that I should be careful.

"Man, it's so much damn pussy out there. They just throw it to you."

I planned to bob and weave from both the pussy and the conversation he wanted to have relating to it. He promptly added, "But man, don't get married. Just hit-and-run." Uncle Terry asked if I was going to sleep, but he didn't care to hear the answer because he already had a request: "Bring ya ass outside and meet my people." I wasn't sure what these people were going to look like, given that, before entering my room, Uncle Terry had boasted to Marcus about how he still got "young hoes" of around twenty-one years old.

Outside, I saw a woman with a weave on top of a weave and gold teeth. (No judgment from me on that. I'm from Houston. Who *doesn't* have gold teeth?) I did wonder about the other girl, who had nails as long as the ones Coko from SWV used to wear, though. I was curious to know if she could claw the shit out of me if I offered one foul look. I leaned toward an empathetic yes and that she had the edge because, even standing a few feet away from me, her thumb could reach my cornea. I also briefly wondered if she owned a bidet, but just as soon realized that it wasn't any of my business.

I don't remember their names. I'm not convinced Uncle Terry does either. Lovely ladies, though. I hope everyone had a good time.

Terry let me go and I crawled back into bed, where I texted Lauren and thanked her for lovingly giving me the push to leave home and truly pursue my dreams—a friend and a roof included.

———

Upon my arrival in LA, I realized that the four-bedroom apartment came with a bit of an asterisk. The place as a whole was indeed huge and cheap, but, as far as bedrooms go, my room was more like a teensy office where you could fit a mattress. But it was better than sleeping at my mama's house!

The place was in Koreatown. K-town wasn't exactly one of LA's finest attractions. It sure wasn't the safest. One of my new roommates informed me that a couple months prior to my moving in, someone had died right around the corner from our building during a gang initiation. Apparently, the victim was set on fire on the sidewalk. I knew what being held at gunpoint was like. Someone who lived up the street from me dying at the hands of another was also not anomalous to my background. But, uh, someone being set on fire on the sidewalk? That actually did make me regret not learning how to keep a blade under my tongue that one time this girl led a demonstration in ninth grade during Algebra I.

It was not lost on me how despite living in Koreatown, I rarely if ever spotted a Korean in our part of Koreatown. I would have described this area as "diet hood" or "hood zero." My neighborhood in Houston was more overt in letting you know that were in the hood. Angelenos: forever dedicated to appearing too cool at all times.

So, yes, a little perplexing at first, but I thought, "I ain't new to this, I'm true to this." Thus it didn't take long for me to survey my surroundings and learn the basics: knowing which streets were safe to frequent and which ones probably weren't the wisest choices to venture to after certain hours; clocking that the house across the street from us might be a good place to get drugs, but never forgetting how that was none of my business. Unfortunately, there was a jolly round fellow across the street who lived in that very building who routinely smiled and waved at me whenever he spotted me en route to the gym or the grocery store. I guessed maybe he wanted me to be his boo thang? He had Desi Arnaz's smile and Nino Brown's business sense. As he was the resident drug dealer of the block, I supposed both qualities were perceived as strengths.

Outside of gawking at me as if I were scrumptious when topped with horseradish, he never actually bothered me. He just stared, albeit profusely, at times. He didn't put fear into my heart. I felt more along the lines of, *You make my dick as cold as the temps scientists wish would stabilize at the Arctic so half of coastal America won't eventually wash away.* Yeah.

Besides, if the white hipsters in the next building over were allowed to huddle up and sing their soft-rock songs at all hours of the night without the threat of violence, I assumed the area was safe enough so long as I avoided certain sidewalks. Not to mention, again, that I'd lived in far worse settings than this. What really mattered the most to me was that the apartment itself had all of the qualities every twentysomething on an intense budget who didn't want to sleep on the street looked out for: cheap and decent. The room may have been the size of a Happy Meal box, but at least the box was in California instead of Texas.

After a few months, the friend who had graciously invited me into her home turned out to be land's answer to Ursula the Sea Witch. She became cold and distant, and our once-beautiful friendship soured as time went on. We made up years later, and no matter what, I'll always love and cherish her, but that was not what I felt at the time. At the time I was like, yo, you encouraged me to come out here only to treat me like you want to run me over with your Corolla—twice, if no one is present to stop you from putting your car in reverse.

I assumed her frustrations were rooted in the fact that she had abandoned her well-paying job in banking to pursue her dream of being a singer. She now found herself with little money and struggling to make ends meet. We were both pursuing our passions, but regrettably, we were not the cheerleaders each other could have used in those darker moments.

Still, me being a recent LA transient, she was the only good friend I had in the city. All the people I cared about had either remained in Houston or had already relocated to New York after college. My initial plan had been to join them there, but I had ended up on the left coast—lonely as hell.

Fortunately, I forged a friendship with Shani. Shani was a girl whom I "met" through an Internet message board I had wasted far too much time on over the years. This would include debating whether or not Rihanna had stolen Fefe Dobson's old clothes and clippers when she relaunched herself with the *Good Girl Gone Bad* album. Back then, I used to wonder whether or not Rihanna needed to be deported. (Fret not, for I have thoroughly repented for my sins since then.)

I used to think the idea of meeting someone from the Internet was a foolproof way of having your mother awakened in the middle of the night by a call confirming your untimely slaughter. However, you just can't ignore the kind of bond you strike with a person over your shared devotion to Beyoncé.

Shani had wanted to meet me as soon as she found out we were now living in the same city. I kept making excuses for why we couldn't get together. I was far too afraid. Not of her stabbing me to death with a plastic fork from Church's Chicken (their forks were especially pointy) or anything like that. I didn't want to meet *any* new people at this point in time. That would have likely resulted in most people's first impressions of me being that I was the worst sort of LA transient cliché: broke and immobile.

I arrived in Los Angeles with only one freelance job that paid $1,500 a month. I also had the nerve to show up in LA without a car. Going to Los Angeles without a car is like going into a steakhouse without any teeth and without a dentures connect—only even more nerve-racking. Fortunately, soon after my arrival, two additional writing gigs presented themselves, and I started saving for a car.

In the meantime, I rode the bus. If you want to learn how to give up on humanity, ride the bus in LA. The only other entity that makes me want to immediately abandon hope in mankind is a public restroom where you quickly learn how few people wash their damn hands. On top of the bus being crammed full of people who needed to better familiarize themselves with manners and strong deodorant, it was also a wonderfully shitty way to get around the city.

Whenever I recall the days of riding the bus in LA, folks quickly hit me back with, "What about Uber? Lyft?" I moved to Los Angeles on the day Barack Hussein Obama was sworn in as president. (Literally every other Negro flying that day was heading to DC, while I was moving to Los Angeles to watch the inauguration on TV.) This was 2009. There was no such thing as Uber. You had your feet and you had the bus, or the subway that no LA native seemed to know existed.

So, yeah, I was reluctant to tell someone I hadn't met before *As much as I'd love to hang out tonight, I don't know how to get to the suggested location by bus, and by the time we're done I'll need a cab ride I can't afford.* These sorts of musings were appreciated only on the East Coast.

Months later, around my birthday, I finally admitted to Shani that I had no car, and thus no big birthday plans. Actually, no birthday plans at all. Ever kind and sweetly relentless, she offered to pick me up on my birthday and take me to the Improv for a show. She was super cute—long hair that looked to be from the finest scalps found in New Delhi. Oh, and the boobs. She had really huge, round boobs. Close your eyes and take that all in if such a type is your thing.

When she arrived, she had a six-pack of cupcakes from Crumbs in tow. Not many people were willing to spend twenty-four dollars on a person they were meeting face-to-face for the first time.

Shani told me that night she had been reading my blog, *The Cynical Ones*, back when it was nothing more than random rants posted on Myspace. She said all the nice things a writer with a dream wanted to hear: that I was funny, special, and that she could see me going very far in my career. She couldn't see a damn thing at night because she was halfway blind, but she saw me being successful in the future and eating red velvet in the moment. Cupcakes and compliments produced a friendship. It was one that teetered on being one-sided—at least when it came to the bill. I was grateful but really uneasy with Shani's generosity.

She would insist on paying, and I would feel guilty for allowing it. I wasn't good with accepting generosity. I wasn't proud of that, but I was not raised to expect anything from anyone outside of immediate family members, and I wasn't even good asking *them* for anything. My guilt translated into declined invitations to continue hanging out. Several declines, actually; I just knew that if I didn't have the money, or had it but needed to save it, it was best to keep myself in that small room. Shani was only being nice, of course, but I continued to feel as if I were an undeserving charity case. What also got to me was the realization that I needed to return the favor and treat her.

She was into those restaurants where celebrities or quasi celebs would call paparazzi to purposely show up and photograph them so they could end up on TMZ, blogs, and social media. In their minds, this made them seem important. I found it to be like taking the taint of desperation and rubbing it all over your face. I got that it was some folks' business model, but it was stupid all the same. (Somewhere, though, some paparazzo person is like, "But you be looking, though!")

In any event, knowing my audience, I invited her to dinner at one of those spiffy restaurants people in LA liked to harp about eating at. Shani accepted, but naturally still had to pick me up because it would be a few more months before I finally had my own ride. We went to Crustacean, a European-Vietnamese restaurant in Beverly Hills that boasted about being the place to "walk on water." They mean walk over a fountain. I suppose if Jesus didn't trademark the phrase, it's legally available for others to use, but I don't blame him if he saw that, flipped his bang, and laughed. The restaurant was hailed for its garlic noodles. I never liked the cheaper, heart-attack-inducing ramen noodles that came in a package, so I was even less interested in trying this wealthier, highfalutin cousin.

As Shani sat there browsing the menu while I contemplated accidentally falling on purpose in order to get a free meal, a loud and very large man in a Fila tracksuit approached our table as if we had motioned him over.

Mr. Fila Tracksuit asked Shani, "Are y'all from LA?"

There's a reason why parents tell their kids, "Don't talk to strangers," but, unfortunately, Shani loved talking to strangers and would do so whenever the opportunity presented itself. No matter where we were, if someone said the weather was nice (it was always nice in LA—even when it rained, it was still nicer than rain elsewhere), she'd manage to end up talking to the person about how their high school quarterback had stage-IV colon cancer and how the entire class was grief-stricken. I used to be that way too. Back in high school, two of my close friends, Kim and Shilisa, joked about how I would have full-on conversations with folks I had just met. There was a difference, though: strangers talked to me, but even though I had a slick mouth on me, I was Southern, and thus polite. Shani revealed her native status, while I made clear that I was from Houston. Literally a second later, Mr. Fila asked me if I knew someone named Brad Ford. I said no, and Fila screamed, "You from Houston and you'on know Brad Ford? What you, a medical student or something?"

I had no idea what one had to do with the other.

I informed Fila that I was actually a writer. He immediately decided to grab a chair and sit down. Who had told him to sit down? Not me.

Why hadn't I just said I was an unemployed chronic masturbator instead?

Telling someone in Los Angeles that you're a writer can yield a number of results. The first might easily be skepticism. Social media has made it easier than ever for people to present what is arguably still a hobby as their profession. Those people who post shots of their butt cheeks on Snapchat or Instagram run through a few filters and captioned with a camera emoji and some person's name? Yeah, meet Jourdan Dunn and Annie Leibovitz. And there are so many "stylists" out there who literally have one client: themselves. Granted, a writer is anyone who writes. The same goes for anyone else who's starting with a dream and pushing to make it their main source of income. I respect and support you. That aside, I write for a living, and even now, when I tell people I'm a writer, I'm sometimes met with pushback along the lines of, "Sure, but how do you eat?"

Another response could be one of pity, because, well, who wants to be a writer in an era when people can't even be burdened to type out "Happy Birthday" in full on social media anymore?

Then there's curiosity. "Who do you write for? What sort of writing do you do?" You must choose your answers wisely in order to avoid the moment when the person starts wondering to themselves, "What can that person do for me?"

Suddenly I felt that a red dart was being aimed at my forehead.

Fila seemed to possess a large amount of self-esteem. It was evident in the fact that he spent twenty minutes talking about his life to a couple of strangers who showed not a lick of genuine interest in what he had to say. It was my own fault for remembering the rule about respecting my elders. That was dumb, because fuck this rude old man. I was also wrong for making a sincere effort to try to control my ever-expressive face. Nature determined me to be the type of person who looked at you stupid the second you displayed such behavior. I had tried to go against the natural order, and Fila was my punishment.

After a while I started to tune him out. Not completely, of course. I needed to know just what level of crazy I was dealing with. As he kept rambling he pulled out two IDs from his wallet.

One had an address that Shani later explained to me was located in some part of LA far worse than where I was. The other ID had some address in Beverly Hills. Why was he telling us any of this? (To this day, I'm still waiting on Scooby Doo and the Mystery Machine to email their findings.)

Fila went on and on. He was a motormouth with a fresh tune-up. He talked about how rich he was. How he had a house in Manhattan. How he had first arrived in LA on a Greyhound bus with twenty cents in his pocket. How he could walk into what he described as "this fine establishment" in a Fila tracksuit. If only the 1990s had kept this man in the decade he belonged in.

In between all of his ranting he repeatedly asked me if I wanted to make money—mumbling something about 35 percent and Paramount.

Initially, I assumed that if I let this crazy motherfucker talk to me for a few minutes, he would eventually go away. But then several minutes went by. Maybe it was only seven minutes, but it felt like forever. Squared.

After a while, I started to realize that this Fila-tracksuit-wearing fucker smelled like Kool cigarettes and more than likely had spent the previous two hours of the night tongue-kissing a bottle of Crown Royal. Probably the maple version, because he was nasty and constantly thought of bacon.

When he had first sat down, I had gotten the sense that he assumed I was dating Shani. I must have spoken or gestured in a more detectable way, because all of a sudden Fila stopped midsentence to ask me, "Are you a homosexual?"

"Yes, as long as women still come with vaginas."

"Does my straightness make you uncomfortable?"

Well, this was different. Usually it was the other way around—the straight person professing his discomfort at a gay person. Was I supposed to be flattered by this line of questioning? But the answer to his question was no. His straightness wasn't the irritant; his existence itself was.

This was the part of the one-sided discussion when I pulled my glass of water closer to me. Fila quipped, "Oh, my man, I'm talking over your water. From the bottom of my heart I am so sorry."

A simple "my bad" would've sufficed, but in any case, that wasn't why I had pulled the glass closer to me. Sensing an attitude at this point, I started to wonder if this crazy-ass man was going to swing on me. I needed to be prepared just in case he tried it. I might have to bash that glass in his face and start swinging.

It finally hit me that Fila wasn't going to leave the table of his own accord. I was being way too polite, which allowed him to get way too comfortable. I was shocked he didn't order an appetizer before we did. Then again, he didn't have a chance to. Our waitress had left us alone for quite some time. When she finally did come back, he told her, "Nah, they're not ready to order."

Man, fuck this.

"Yes we are, homie—hold on."

I motioned to the waitress to come back over while beginning to grip that glass of water more firmly. Finally, we were able to order our meals: saddity salmon, bougie crab legs, and those damn noodles everyone was fawning over.

"It's time for you to go, sir."

"'Sir'?!"

Another problem: Southern manners.

Being civilized clearly wasn't going to work.

Also not working was Fila repeatedly touching my arm while he spoke to me. I guess my gayness didn't bother his straightness.

After finishing his soliloquy about why his life ought to be made into a movie, Fila kept pressing me: "Now, what do you say? Do you want to make money?!"

"I'm okay. Good luck to you and your book-deal-movie thing."

Followed with: "No disrespect, man, but you've been here for a minute, and I'm with my friend and we're trying to enjoy our dinner."

Fila: "Well, fine! Die poor!"

Say what?

I had been banished into poverty over declining the offer to write this unidentified man's autobiography and biopic.

"You try to help people out, and look how they treat you. Fine, be poor. Die poor. Your problem!"

Coincidentally, I was being told this as I was developing the fear of such a fate. Los Angeles was the perfect place to let this sort of anxiety blossom, given everyone's penchant to parade their wealth. Even the theme of this dinner was my modest way of showing appreciation for kindness and generosity to someone in a much better position than mine.

Offended by the writing guy from Houston who had the nerve to not know who the unidentified but seemingly awesome Brad Ford was, Fila huffed and puffed and finally got his ass the hell away from our table.

Our waitress came back with our food. Sensing the hostility in the air, it dawned on her what had just happened.

"Wait, did you know that guy?"

"NO!"

You damn fool.

"I thought he was your father the way he was yelling at you."

Now, my looks have been described as a fake-ass Chris Brown and a knockoff Chico DeBarge. By contrast, Fila looked like "What if Danny Glover lived on an all-pork-and-cigarette diet?" Like father, like son?

The manager appeared, and Fila—still lingering around the premises, likely searching for another Black victim in the restaurant—was escorted out. The manager apologized and offered us a free dessert. The dessert was bland as hell. Considering they let a stranger in nylon terrorize me at the table, they could've at least offered us some liquor. Hell, I would've settled for complimentary crab cakes. A Southern restaurant sure would've given us some, and maybe even suggested we drive to the Walmart after and get us a gun and some of those frozen Tyson chicken tenders on sale.

In the midst of Fila's fury, Shani and I didn't pick up on the live entertainment at the restaurant. I'm not sure if this was to our benefit, but the jazz vocalist and pianist—both white—started performing a spirited rendition of "Wade in the Water."

Wade in the Water
Wade in the Water, children
Wade in the Water
God's gonna trouble the Water

Yes, white people in an Asian fusion restaurant were performing a Negro spiritual. If any Negro spirits had been awakened by their performance, it would have likely been only to bitch-slap them both in disgust.

When the bill came, the dinner totaled $120 plus tip.

As Shani reached for her wallet, I reminded her that this was my treat.

"Are you sure?"

"Yes," I said hastily.

A crazy man, forecasts of poverty, and a poorly advised song selection combined with food that wasn't remarkably special notwithstanding, I had promised to pay for this dinner, and I intended to keep my word. This meal encapsulated my entire outlook on Los Angeles: a pretty place full of kind natives largely overshadowed by soulless transients looking to score. I have no idea what happened to that old man, but I hope that Fila tracksuit of his caught on fire.

Learning How to Ho and Date and Failing at Both

*H*aving paranoia about sex did not mean that I lived a completely asexual experience. For me, there was the ideal situation in which I desired to have sex in terms of penetration—someone I cared about deeply—and the reality that during immense fits of sexual frustration, I needed a release. Sometimes this meant engaging in sexual acts that assuaged some of that unsettling tension but left me feeling as though I was too loose with my own standards. Most times, however, I went on dates with the intent to forge meaningful connections that would give way to the ideal scenarios for sexual eruptions. Unfortunately, I forgot to keep one thing in mind: men are fucking awful.

I. 2007.

I assumed he was biracial, because despite clearly being of Asian descent, he had braids and wore a grill, and his name was Trevonte.

He didn't necessarily have Jackson 5 nostrils, but they were at least B2K nostrils, so there was a legit reason not to have a definitive answer on his racial makeup. And again, his name was Trevonte. Not to be completely stereotypical, but Trevonte is the kind of name that screams Black. For the record, I'm not a racist working in human resources who sees a name like Trevonte and promptly deletes the résumé over fears that upon being hired, he'll show up carrying a huge tub of Lawry's seasoned salt and sprinkle it all around his cubicle to mark his territory as he quietly plans the race war on company time. In fact, I've mulled naming a set of twins I'll create with the help of science "Destiny's Child" and "Jodeci." (Then again, there are quite a few 1990s babies with the name Jodeci, and perhaps I oughta go with another R & B group of that era like Troop or Silk.) I remain undecided on that, but to be clear, while I have no problems with names that scream Black-Black-Black, I do expect someone named Trevonte to at least have one parent of Negro descent.

We met at a gay Black club in Houston called 20/20. It was Saturday night, so virtually every gay Black man who was a clubgoer would frequent it—yet another reason to assume Trevonte was a racial and ethnic concoction like Tiger Woods. I was back in Houston, miserable and trying to figure out how in the hell I had ended up back in my hometown after spending all that time and money in college trying to live anywhere else but Houston. Going to the club and getting drunk out of my mind was a coping mechanism. I also went because my sex life was nonexistent, and that club was a good venue for me to work out some of my sexual frustration. I wasn't having sex, but I did feel up boys, get felt up myself, and, on occasion, exchange numbers with someone who ideally might become someone I would get to know, fall for, and, when I felt comfortable, consummate the relationship with. I had been at 20/20 for hours, and it was nearing the time for me to begin drinking a whole lot of water, chill for a spell in the parking lot of the club with the other gays who didn't know when to go home, and make a pit stop at Whataburger before going back home and purposely forgetting everything that just happened.

The club was massive. It had three levels, though only two functioned as places where everyone actually partied. The line began on the ground floor, but you had to walk up steps to have your ID checked and to pay to get in. Upon entry, you were on the second level, which was a sizable space in and of itself, but there were two ramps on both the left and right sides that you took you down to the massive dance floor. And there was a very large stage area where men would occasionally perform. Either they would perform as drag queens or set up their own impromptu dance troupe and twerk it out while everyone was drunk or high out of their minds. Trevonte was sitting in the middle of that stage surrounded by a sea of Black boys. He made eye contact with me—possibly because he thought I might've been my brother—but that was about it. I was used to men not approaching me and having to make the first move, so I walked over. I introduced myself, I told him that he was cute, and we exchanged numbers.

Upon texting, I learned that he was not mixed but Filipino. I should have known better. This was Houston, Texas, where braids and grills were as common as men in the hood going up and down the street on horseback. Houston has always been incredibly diverse, but there is a bit of what some would describe as "ratchetness" to be found in city residents regardless of their socioeconomic status or racial background. Whether or not they have any inherent anti-Blackness may be another story, though.

I was complimentary and flirtatious, but I often had a habit of sometimes speaking a wee bit too loosely. When I found out he was Filipino rather than being the by-product of at least one Black parent, I said, "Oh, you're like an Asian Paul Wall." Paul Wall was a white rapper from Houston who had immersed himself in the culture well enough to where he could bring potato salad to a cookout and Black folks present wouldn't inherently question whether he put raisins in it (he had a Black wife, so she'd likely step in and save the day). One could only discern the tone of texting to a certain point, but I got the sense Trevonte didn't love the comparison despite my actually having spotted him singing along to Paul Wall in the club that same night. He let it slide, though, because after a few more days of texting back and forth, we finally set up a date.

He told me to meet him at a sushi spot I understood to be frequented by all kinds but on Fridays was populated heavily by Black people. It had a lengthy happy hour that went well into the night, with heavily discounted food and drinks. It also had both a large area for dining and an equally big area that served as more of a lounge. Guess which night Trevonte picked. He did so partially because he had a relative there who worked as a bartender, one who would be quite generous with his gig's available alcohol. Considering that I had only recently started freelance writing and was learning to save money to move away, in addition to developing the skill set to efficiently harass accounts-payable departments to get my money in a timely manner, I was not going to turn down a date with a cute boy who had lots of muscles and tats, with free drinks to boot. After all, my broke ass was driving my mama's car there anyway.

We met at the bar, and as soon as I sat down, he asked me if I wanted something to eat. I told him no. I had not eaten all day. I had a high tolerance when it came to drinking, but that was only if you factored in food first. Given that I had nothing in my stomach before I was due to drink a lot with this guy, my answer should have been an emphatic yes. But no, not me. I wanted to be cute and drink. For a while, we simply talked. I learned that he was a junior at the University of Houston, majoring in criminal justice with the goal of going to law school and becoming a lawyer. I told him about my time at Howard, what I had done, and what I still planned to do once I escaped again.

Then he asked if I wanted to take a shot. I said sure, so we took a shot. And then another. And then another. And then another. Suddenly, it had become some sort of competition. In between the shots, we ordered more drinks. I lost count of how many we took, but I do know in between those shots, my body turned into a placeholder for his hands, and I responded in kind. He asked me if I had any plans afterward, and upon my saying no, he suggested we link up with his cousin and the guy she was with and all hang out. I agreed, but after tipping his brother and standing up, it dawned on me just how drunk I was. Keeping in line with a night of questionable choices, rather than take the elevator down to the car, I went down the steps, petrified of falling down and knocking out my two big, buck front teeth. Although Trevonte had driven himself, he noticed how drunk I was and said I could leave my car there and he would drive as we all hung out for a few more hours. By then, I would sober up, he would take me back to my car, and we could go on our merry ways. He didn't seem drunk at all. That was probably because he had eaten food, drunk a lot of water, and behaved like an adult who wanted to have his cognitive functions working. I handed him the keys but told him to wait a second. I needed to pee. I didn't go back into the restaurant, which was only a few feet away. No, I whipped my dick out in front of a closed Victoria's Secret and pissed directly on it. Highland Village featured an upscale shopping center down the street from the Galleria, another upscale shopping center in Houston that was home to many fancy restaurants and a grocery store I would aptly describe as "the nice rich white folks' grocery store to get meat from." And I was pissing outside of it in front of the store where you buy nice panties and body lotions.

As Trevonte was driving me to wherever we were going, he made a pit stop at a gas station. He told me that I needed to get some air, so I did. I sat outside on the curb for a few minutes and called one of my friends as he went inside to buy whatever. Unbeknownst to my drunk ass, I was sitting on a fire-ant bed. For several minutes. It didn't hit me that I was being eaten alive by an army of ants until I started to feel them at the tippy top of my back as they raced to get to my neck and finish me off. I leaped up in agony and started to scream "What the fuck?" It was Trevonte who noticed the ants and told me to take off my shirt. In gentlemanly fashion, he took off his shirt and then took off his undershirt and started to try to knock them off me with it. I wasn't certain that we got them all off, but I didn't feel like I was a buffet offering anymore, so we got back into the car and ended up at some sort of motel.

I wasn't anticipating that we'd have sex on date number one. Sure, we did have chemistry and I was perpetually horny, but we hadn't discussed that. Yet I was drunk and needed to spend a few hours sobering up. I had no idea whose room this was or what part of town I was in. As soon as I got there, I immediately got into the shower to wash off whatever ants might've still been on my body. Trevonte quickly joined me. He didn't have a single ounce of body fat on him, whereas I was worried about whether or not I had done enough push-ups to make certain that I didn't have man boobs. After the shower, we got in the bed. Moments later, his cousin and some Black man with locs joined us. They were on one bed and we were on the other.

Was I at the intersection of a family reunion and a sex party? Yet despite the setting being primed for drunken sex, we did not have it. Between the shower, and the water I had started downing in the car and continued drinking in this spot, things were becoming clearer.

So, did we roll around awhile? Yes, but we didn't have any form of sex. He did try to slide himself into my mouth, but I had already put too many things down my throat that night, so I was tapped out. I let him finish on me as a compromise. It was the least I could do.

By the time I looked around, I noticed that Trevonte's cousin and her Black man were both gone. I put my clothes back on, grabbed my car keys, and left. Once I got home, my mom was already up getting ready for her 6:00 a.m. shift at the hospital. It was a good thing she was, because the pain that came from all of those ant bumps across my stomach and my back was surfacing, and it was excruciating. My mom looked at me in shock and horror, wondering how this could have happened. I left off the drunk part of the explanation. Regardless, ever the nurse, my mom pulled out some creams and other medication and told me what to do. While the pain went away, the scarring from all that scratching I was told not to do was setting in.

If not for the power of cocoa butter, who knows what would have become of my stomach. As for Trevonte, we never had a second date. We texted each other about having had a good time, but it quickly fizzled out. That was probably for the best. I would leave for Los Angeles in the coming months, but more importantly, on a first date with him, I had gotten too drunk to drive, peed on a fancy panty store, sat on an ant bed, and then let him bust on me. And in hindsight, it was likely that Trevonte wasn't his damn name and I was being fetishized. The thought had crossed my mind at one point because he did try to use "nigga" near the end and I immediately said, "Oh, we're not doing that."

I had scars for months across my abdomen. Bless my heart.

II. 2007.

Months after Trevonte, the dark scars across my stomach began to fade, and I met Michael, who worked at one of the nicer grocery store chains in Houston. They were nicer because they were all primarily located in white neighborhoods. I lived in a Black neighborhood, and directly behind my neighborhood was another neighborhood largely populated by Latinos. The grocery stores nearest both our hoods at the time were *fine*, but one could easily gauge who was blessed and highly favored when it came to food. We shopped at all of them, but more often than not, my mom would pick up meat from the nicer stores (unless she fried catfish and shrimp and we went to the store near us that had live seafood, like the real ones they are). She never directly made mention of it, but one thing I learned from her shopping habits was that simply living in an area considered to be the "inner city" did not mean we had to be eating food of lower quality. As I got older, I noticed the price points between the grocery stores weren't all that different. What was different, however, was the quality of meat. The meat at the grocery stores in white neighborhoods was better than the meat found in the Black ones—

once I bought ground turkey at one of the Black ones and was keeled over in pain for three days—so I tried to shop there instead. The grocery store Michael worked at was about a fifteen-minute drive, very little driving time by Houston's standards, so if the difference was between meat I could trust and meat that could have me dying decades before I intended to, I went with the former.

Judgmental folks have scrunched up their faces when I say this, but I have found grocery shopping to be relaxing, because it provides me with the perfect opportunity to turn on my headphones and twerk down the aisles while looking for discounted tortilla chips. (The kind that either say "blue corn" or "multigrain" so you'll have less guilt about inhaling the entire bag while watching *The Real Housewives of Atlanta* because you've convinced yourself that because the chips aren't fried, they're healthier for you.) When I go to a grocery store, I normally zone out, bop aggressively, and rummage through the chicken to find the perfect package of wings: bountiful but not so pricey that you end up saying, "Fuck this. I'mma get Popeyes because it's the same price with less work. Shit." The grocery store, much like the gym, constituted *me time*. I was back in Houston and feeling defeated, and when I wasn't working and plotting to move the hell away all over again during most weekdays, I'd down way too much caffeine, hit the gym, and follow that with a trip to the grocery store.

I noticed Michael a few times before we spoke to each other, but I didn't pursue him. He looked young. Not young to the point that if I spoke to him, an undercover police officer would jump out of the meat freezer and tackle me, but still. Alas, while I was stripper-kicking in the chip aisle, he asked me if I needed anything. Despite being sweaty as hell and a bit perturbed that he had interrupted me during my favorite part of Crime Mob's "Rock Yo Hips," I thanked him for offering to help but noted that I was fine. He apologized for "bothering me," though after noticing his name tag, I told him that my name was Michael, too. The Michael that wasn't me smiled about that, but considering this Michael hated small talk, I told him to have a good night and went about my way. I turned around, and sure enough, he was still looking at me. I left the grocery store without the chips and went to Taco Cabana, located in the same parking lot as that grocery store, and proceeded to blow my workout.

Once you meet someone, you tend to keep running into them—especially if, you know, they work there and shit. I ran into Michael multiple times over the next month. I would speak to him, but I kept the conversation at minimum. Gradually, the length of our conversations extended, and we started to learn a few things about each other. He had just finished high school and was planning to go to college in Louisiana. I told him that I had just finished college. I wasn't sure what prompted it—a hand motion or some other mannerism from me—but he felt compelled to randomly note that he liked women.

"Oh, cool. That's nice."

Translation: I don't want you, dude. Calm your dick and delusions of grandeur.

Was he cute? Yes.

Is that why I talked to him when I spotted him in the grocery store? I considered it a bonus. An aesthetic treat as part of my karma for being a polite Southern man.

Did I go to the store sometimes hoping to run into him? Only once, so it shouldn't be held against me. Shut up.

Regardless, as nice as he was to look at, I didn't care that much about him. If had I never seen him again after that evening, I would have been perfectly fine. (I hate when seemingly straight men do that. Not every gay man is concerned about you. We often do not care, and can be just as tribal as the breeders.) So, I didn't need the disclaimer that he had a girlfriend because I wasn't in the grocery aisles cruising.

As fate would have it, it turned out that he did have some nominal sexual interest in men that he had not yet explored. This was confirmed the next time I saw him at the grocery store, when he found me and asked for my number. My immediate response was that I was a little old for him. He was eighteen, about to turn nineteen (I asked for ID because you will not catch the kid slipping), and I was a smooth twenty-three years old by then. That wasn't a big gap in actuality, but it was in mind-set. I had already finished college, and he was about to start at some school in Louisiana playing basketball. No matter my age, since coming out, I'd noticed that I tended to attract younger men. Part of that was people tending to assume I was younger than I actually was. The other and more indicting part of this pattern was that my apparent youthfulness could also register as sexual immaturity. Or maybe because I was older, he assumed I was more experienced and could help him figure his own self out. Whatever the case, I didn't think we would have much to talk about. But this didn't matter, since conversation wasn't at the center of either of our interests.

After texting for a few days, he told me that he was getting off work soon and asked if I wanted to link up. His car was in the shop, so I picked him up from work and we "hung out." He didn't live far from the store, so he suggested we drive around a bit before making a stop in some park. After parking, we took off our seatbelts and engaged in no more than two minutes of empty conversation before he reached for my dick. Once he was finished, he asked me to return the favor.

Now, there are some people in this world who love sucking dick. I am not one of them. That's not to say I can't perform well ('cause someone fine as hell could be reading this) when duty calls, but I can be selfish as shit when it comes to blowing other men. Most dicks are ugly; therefore I reserve going down for people I sincerely care about (or if you're really really really fine and that spurs my generous spirit). This was not the case for Michael, whom I did not know and who had already proven to be a bit of a liar. He made the most pitiful face in the world, and I guess since my dick was the first one he had ever had in his mouth, I begrudgingly returned the favor.

"Damn, my girl don't even do it like this."

Your who, *nigga?*

Why was I not surprised that he had a girlfriend? I didn't know the young lady, of course, but apparently she didn't give good head, and I imagined she didn't touch his ass in a way that prompted further internal inquiries about his primary sexual attraction.

The tryst ended abruptly as some police officer drove into the parking lot, presumably to check out why some random car was there that late at night. Not trying to pay tribute to George Michael's arrest record, I told Michael to zip up and then took him home. He texted me that he had had a good time and that we should link again soon.

The next morning, I woke up and saw various scrapes across my dick. The lil' bastard had braces! Was this karma for the scrapes I had left on Jordan years before? I took myself to CVS to get some triple antibiotic ointment.

There was no next time. Funny; after those months of always seeing him at his job after leaving the gym, I ran into him one Saturday morning *at* the gym. He was with some older man, and while I knew better than to run up on him like, "SO WE GON' FUCK NEXT TIME OR NAH?" I did at least try to say hello. I couldn't even reach the "o" in "hello" because younger Michael sprinted like hell away from me. If he hadn't gotten his cardio in before that, he for sure got it racing away from me.

I texted to ask if there was a problem. Radio silence. I tried to text him a few days after that. Again, no response. Then it hit me: oh, this dude truly *is* conflicted. That fear in his eyes looked familiar. He enjoyed me, but he wasn't ready to face what that meant. At the time, I thought it was my fault. That once again I had repelled some man. But that was not the pattern to be concerned with. The pattern that required my real attention was my turning to sexually confused men for sexual exploration. It was like my turning to someone who can't figure out "there," "they're," and "their" to edit your essay.

I would have had sex with Michael if the opportunity had presented itself, but it didn't because he was afraid. His fear of me made me more fearful about my own sexual exploration. God, what if he had hit a vein with that metal contraption wired to his mouth? Could I have bled to death? Can you imagine my funeral?

We lost our wannabe whorish but nonetheless Christian brother Michael Joseph Arceneaux to an adulterous act performed by a curious sodomite. I don't know if he went to hell, but let us pray that God had more mercy on Michael's soul than that other Michael had on his penis.

Several years later, I saw Michael at a gay bar called Bayou City. I was home for the holidays, and while I love my straight cousins, I wanted the company of other sissies dancing to music I could only hear at a club back home. Michael looked older and, to me, much better. He didn't notice me until a little later. I was leaving the bathroom and going back to the bar, because more brown liquor felt necessary. Then our eyes met. He didn't look afraid anymore, and from the looks of it, had a boyfriend with him. All we did was give each other a nod as a greeting. As much as I had resented watching someone literally run away from the sight of me, I understood it. With age came experience.

Speaking of, now that he was free of braces, no funeral would have to be planned.

III. 2010.

We met outside the Abbey. It was 2:00 a.m., so Los Angeles had effectively shut down because the city's nightlife was useless without alcohol unless you had weed and access to an after-hours spot worth your time. That night I was in possession of neither, so it was time to drive my ass to Jack in the Box, devour a Bacon Ultimate Cheeseburger value meal with curly fries and a Coke (each jumbo-sized), shower, and take my ass to sleep. As I was walking out, I locked eyes with a guy whom, a few hours prior, I had seen while in the midst of complaining to my friends for the umpteenth time that I missed the gay bars in the South because techno music made me question the existence of God. He was incredibly attractive. If I were an A & R exec, I would sell him as a man who had the appearance of a heartthrob R & B singer but lacked the talent to be one: we could sell him to audiences as a semicompetent rapper who could get girls and gays to monetarily support his musical career for a few years. A light-skinned version of Chingy, if you will.

His name was An'toine. (I'm not for sure why the name needed to be separated with that apostrophe, but I don't want to disrespect the man's mama, so I'll leave it alone.) He went by that name, his middle name, and a hyphenated last name that consisted of both his parents' last names. I applaud the progressiveness there, but one of his parents had a last name as long as the space between New York and Los Angeles. I bet he took all day to sign shit.

He was waiting outside with his friends when we made eye contact for a second time, but as always, it was up to me to do the approaching. So I did, and although he was warm to me, you got the sense that he could be cold to those he didn't want in his periphery. My concerns were heightened once we started to communicate via text. There was a strong whiff of jackass emanating from his messages. The same could be said of the clear signs of stupid. I am no grammar nazi. I don't anticipate anyone writing in complete sentences. I accept people using "u" for "you" or "ur" for "your," and whatever instances of shorthand folks like to use sans the following: "HBU," "WYD," and "HBD." With him, it wasn't so much how he typed but what he said, or was trying to say. You could tell he was more into the superficial than the substantive. It was all too apparent he was more invested in optics than anything else. No wonder he would wriT3 lYk3 tHis. God, a simple "How are you?" from me invited a bowl of alphabet soup in my BlackBerry Bold. It was as if his texts were trying to reach through the screen to warn me, "Don't do this, Arceneaux."

And yet I asked him out anyway. Because he was incredibly attractive, and I wanted some ass. So I went despite having it on good ground that this probably wouldn't work the way I thought it would. Where we chose to eat was a bit of a one-sided negotiation. He was adamant about picking the restaurant, and every single one of his options was ultraexpensive. I didn't mind paying for an expensive meal, nor did I object to paying for the company of someone I had invited out. Did I have it like that? Hell no, but you weren't going to have me looking like I was a cheap-ass. Still, the way he broached the issue was a turnoff. He discussed it with this sense of entitlement coupled with a bitchiness that I found frustrating. *Like, I don't mind taking you where you want to go, but you're acting like an escort, and if that's the case, how much are you? We can get to the point, because, after all, food would get in your way, no?* Having said that, despite getting the sense that he wasn't the sharpest person in the Southern California region from his texts, most of those texts were flirtatious on both ends, so once again, I brushed the signs away.

An'toine ended up picking none of the options he had previously mentioned. Maybe he merely wanted to see if I would be willing to go wherever he wanted. Whatever the case, we ended up at Yard House, some saddity sports bar. I went with an open mind and hoped for the best. That feeling didn't last long. Once we sat in front of each other, the sense I had that he had the capability to be cold was promptly confirmed. He greeted me like I was the uncle who falsely claimed one of his mama's children to cheat on his taxes.

During the get-to-know-each-other portion of the evening, he said, "Wait, you said you're a writer, right? What do you write about?" After giving him the topics and some of the outlets I was writing for, he looked me up and down and snarled, "I don't like to read." My response should have been, *You don't like to read, but you write lengthy-ass Facebook posts as if you're Iyanla Vanzant with a learning disability or a keyboard that barely functions because you spilled a liter of Dr. Pepper on it.*

Who doesn't like to read? This beautiful, empty-headed jackass who liked to dispense passionate, grossly uninformed "life tips" on the Mark Zuckerberg–made platform, apparently.

Yes, it was a pretty shitty thing to respond to a writer by saying "I don't like to read," but at the same time, I didn't give that great of a fuck. If you wanted to be stupid, such was your right.

What insulted me was what happened a few minutes later. My back was turned to the person when he said it, but An'toine declared, "You look just like that dude at the bar." I turned around and looked.

It's impolite to call someone ugly, but it's equally rude to tell a person that they resemble someone you would call a bugawolf in your head.

"I don't look like him."

"Yeah you do."

"I do not look like him, An'toine."

"C'mon, you've got to see it."

"I don't see shit over there but someone's child who doesn't at all look like the one in front of you."

But he kept pressing it.

It's one thing to say you think my profession is a waste of time because the consumption of words is too taxing an ordeal for you and your unimaginative mind, but I'll be damned if you say I mirror a man who appears to be well over a decade older, at least twenty pounds smaller, and looks like the light inside of him got stomped out by three cases of bourbon consumed five years prior. You got me fucked up.

In just under an hour, I had learned An'toine was blind and dumb. Thankfully, he spared me from discovering that he might also be slightly deaf, because he said he had somewhere to be in the morning. He meant his job, but I personally wished that he would drive into the fourth circle of hell. We didn't hug good-bye, and that was perfectly fine. While in the parking lot, I started to entertain the thought of finding a hypnotist to fulfill my mom's desires for me to like vagina, marry one, and make grandchildren with it in the name of the Father, the Son, and the Holy Spirit, because that motherfucker annoyed the everlasting shit out of me. By the time I got inside of my car, I called my friend Kim in Houston. I asked her if it would be okay to run him over. She told me no.

"I know violence is wrong, and I already look like Chris Brown's second cousin to some people, but doesn't he deserve to be hit?"

"Yes, but you can't do that. I don't got no bail money."

Considering how often God behaved like a troll, it was no surprise that I ran into An'toine repeatedly for a few months, and then finally he fizzled away. Two years later, I got a message from him on Facebook Messenger. It was 6:00 a.m. in New York, where I now lived, which meant it was the middle of the night for him back in LA.

"HUB?"

The fuck is that?

Oh, you want to know how I've been? This is why you need to join a book club, damn fool.

After that, he randomly inserted that he was horny. It was the fringes of the day, so I was too. We took the conversation back to text after he sent a picture revealing just how horny he was. I responded by saying I wish I had gotten a chance to get at that when I was in LA.

Me 2 but u was trippin.

By my love of literacy? Supposedly, I was too eager and rushing him to get serious. Serious how? I had no idea what he was talking about and could bet he was confusing me with some other sucker whose time he had also wasted. After masturbating to his videos and pictures, I was finished and told him that if he was ever in New York, he could hit me up and we could finally make something happen. He said "cool" while casually mentioning that I could also fly him to New York.

Hardy har, bitch.

My mistake was that I should have never bothered trying to get to know him on any deeper level. That wasn't how you were supposed to ho. You made your intentions clear and acted accordingly. I knew this fool was a fool only good for fornication, and I gave far too much energy to someone I only could deal with in scenarios centered on ejaculation.

He was a terrible person. Having said that, I know terrible people can be tempting, and despite his being an insulting, rude simpleton who needs to have his eyes examined, I would still fuck. Obviously, it would be a hate fuck. And for my own comfort, I would bring a book and pull a condom out of it.

IV. 2016.

Even after he told me that once upon a time, he'd faced nearly a twenty-five-year sentence for beating the hell out of his ex to the point that he had multiple severe head wounds, I was thinking, "I'd still fuck, though."

We met at a restaurant called Sexy Taco/Dirty Cash in Harlem. Sexy Taco/Dirty Cash sounds like the name of a rapper's mixtape. I know this because the name of my unreleased mixtape is *Cognac and Celexa*. Before the restaurant was called Sexy Taco/Dirty Cash, it was called La Bodega. And before it was called La Bodega, it was called Native. These name changes all happened within the first four years of my living in Harlem. In spite of this, the owner has remained the same. Presumably, he bores easily, and change is a constant in his sphere.

Sexy Taco/Dirty Cash is a rum bar that sells tacos inspired by San Francisco food trucks. This is their description, not mine. I am from Texas, and after living in Los Angeles for a few years, I now know that Tex-Mex is nothing like the Mexican food found in any other region of the country. Like most Texans, I think our way is the best way.

Bryce, the man who almost went to prison for manslaughter, was also from Texas, so we shared this sentiment about Mexican food, and most things generally. He wasn't from the best part— Houston—like me and Beyoncé, but I didn't hold that against him either. People always talk about forgiveness, but we do not always allow people who aren't necessarily monsters but committed monstrous acts the space to sincerely start over. Bryce talked a lot about therapy, anger management, moving to New York, and, pointedly, the ability to now know when to leave a violent relationship. He came across as sincere in changing the course of his life after his self-described "life-changing experience." Bryce also had a Louisiana connection. He was, as one country-ass man who read my name at a midwestern airport once blurted out, "One of them Creoles, ain't you?"

Bryce worked as a hair stylist—primarily taming heads over at the de facto state TV network known as Fox News. When he shared this, I had to make a conscious decision: to ask more questions and potentially sour the mood of this drinks situation or just sit and smile and try to get to know the hottie in front of me.

It had taken a good while for this meeting to happen. I had been talking to Bryce online for well over a month and had decidedly given up on us linking because he didn't seem that interested in me. Then out of the blue on Facebook, he circled back to an invitation beginning to mold in the dark corner of his Messenger inbox to ask, "Are we ever going to get those drinks?" I assumed he was bored, but considering I was being trifling and evading an assignment with a deadline crawling up my leg, I agreed. Another motivating factor was that through my virtual snooping, I had learned a lot about his body by way of his many, many thirst traps posted on Instagram.

It was Bryce who decided that we would meet at Sexy Taco/ Weird, Long Name. He asked for options in Harlem, but with a caveat: "I need a frozen margarita. They're all I drink!" He liked dick and diabetes, I guess.

We met around ten that evening. He had just gotten off work at Murdoch's House of Madness (Clearly), Sexual Harassment (Allegedly), and Propaganda (Obviously). The conversation was going pretty okay until that mention of Fox News came up. Sensing my hesitance to dive deeper into his work, he went, "I know, I know. But I don't have anything to do with that." He surely did not. After all, he did the anchors' hair, he said, not fill their minds with that drivel they spew. For about fifteen minutes, I let him tell stories about various anchors. To the shock of no one, Bill O'Reilly was apparently a racist asshole (and, as we would later learn, an accused sexual predator at the workplace, which led to his ultimate ejection). Somewhat surprising to me, Sean Hannity was "nice." Wasn't that special? "Fuck Sean Hannity" was my response to that new nugget of intel.

Then the now former Fox News anchor Megyn Kelly came up.

While Bryce had learned I was a writer, and a very opinionated one at that, he didn't know how I felt about Kelly, whom he
fancied very much. I hated Megyn Kelly. I was raised not to say that
I hated anyone, but I was also raised to procreate by way of vaginal
sex and holy matrimony. If I could break the rules on that, I could
break the rules on declarations of hatred. I fucking hate Megyn
Kelly. As Bryce went on and on about what a nice woman she was
and how well she treated everyone on set, the forced smile on my
face could no longer handle the weight of pretending I harbored
nothing but disdain for her.

I agreed with Bryce that Megyn Kelly's role in helping oust Roger
Ailes was a courageous act forever worthy of celebration. However,
Megyn Kelly, like Bill O'Reilly, like Sean Hannity, like Tucker Carl-
son, like those morning simpletons on *Fox & Friends*, and like just
about everyone on that network besides Shepard Smith, followed
the Fox News model of stoking racial animus to pander to the old,
white racists who watched the news network in droves. She magni-
fied the New Black Panther Party in ways no sensible newsperson
ever would—because their clout was virtually nonexistent within
the Black community—to the point where journalists decried her
work as a "minstrel show." She was a woman who, in 2015, claimed
that the Obama administration intended to force "too white [and]
too privileged" communities to embrace diversity "whether the
communities want it or not." That same year, Kelly dismissed a DOJ
report that found racial bias and stereotyping within the Fergu-
son, Missouri, police department based on the notion that "there
are very few companies in America, whether they are public or private," where "you won't find any racist emails [or] any inappropriate
comments." The same person who once declared that a speech by

First Lady Michelle Obama played into a "culture of victimization." A woman who invoked racial stereotypes to portray Supreme Court Justice Sonia Sotomayor as temperamental. And the woman who, despicably, described a Black girl needlessly tackled by police at a pool party as "no saint."

Evidence of Kelly's on-air racism was far and wide. I honestly, truly might have gotten over the fact that Bryce had almost cracked the skull of an ex. I could fight, and there was a troupe of folks who would swoop me in if he had a relapse. I could get with him learning to "relax, relate, release" and exhale, shoop, shoop, after a brush with the law. But Megyn Kelly? How could he question all the evidence presented before him? He had her hair looking pretty as she said the ugliest shit about *us*. What about that was not racist and reprehensible?

"I don't think it's fair to call her racist, because you don't know what's in her heart."

Oh, dear God, you are one of those. Whenever there were accusations of racism leveled against someone likely guilty of being a racist, the peanut gallery would come with the retort that it was hard to gauge another person's racism because we didn't know what was in their heart.

I didn't give a fuck what was in her heart. That had nothing to do with whether or not she was racist. There are levels to racism. In the case of Kelly, stoking racial prejudices for professional gain was a racist act. This drinks thing also happened after the 2016 presidential election, so to that end, I thought of Megyn Kelly as the epitome of the 53 percent of white women who voted for that man, Sweet Potato Saddam: a white woman willing to sacrifice the humanity of nonwhites to preserve her privilege and status. She may not have presented herself in the same way as the loud, cantankerous, vile white men with whom she shared prime-time space, but she was guilty of perpetuating the same sins because she delivered the same ugly sentiments about Black people on her breath.

After explaining all of this, all I got back was the sight of this man slurping from his third frozen sugary-ass margarita and the quip, "I disagree." Then he went to the restroom, and as I watched him walk to and from the bathroom, I wondered if my visible annoyance and monologue had killed the mood. Fine, I didn't have to wonder: I had killed the mood. We changed the subject and talked more about each other, but whatever this was, it had pretty much died. Many advise not talking about politics on dates, but he was half Black and it was Megyn Kelly. I have never met a Black person in New York City who greeted the topic of Megyn Kelly with a smile and a gush about her not being so bad. I just assumed he did her hair, offered her a few, "Hey, girl!"s here and there, and then texted his friends like, *I HATE HER.* But when you make assumptions, you sometimes don't get any ass.

I never saw him again. I wonder what he thought of me. Like, even though he was the one with the violent past, did he think I was going to break a glass and scream "Black lives matter!" at him?

I regret nothing.

This Place Is No Sanctuary

As a kid, I had jet-black hair full of curls. I used to routinely twist my hair in the front into a knot. My sister used to always tease in response to this comforting habit: "Quit doing that! You're going to go bald." I would always tell her to stop saying that, as it sparked too intense a fear in me. There were some men and women who were stunning bald, but not once had I ever thought my peanut head would allow a similar beauty for me. The end result was me never, ever wanting to go bald or to give the appearance that I was going bald. I tended to obsess over my hair and was particular about the way I believed it ought to look. These were character traits I definitely shared with my father.

My earliest memory of barbers was my dad's friend JB, who used to cut in a garage: ours or his. I liked JB a lot. Most of my dad's friends were as loud and rowdy as he was, but there were others like JB who were a lot more chill and measured in their behavior— a necessary counterpoint to the magnetic personality of my pops, a man who didn't know how to be still unless he was sleeping. I also liked JB because he would feign being impressed by me repeating phrases like "three-hundred-and-sixty-degree angle." We both knew I had lifted that from professional-wrestling commentators, but encouragement was encouragement. I had met so many of my dad's friends over the years. Some stuck around; many others didn't. JB did not, but I don't recall anyone ever questioning one of his cuts.

After JB, my dad took me up the street to a barbershop located in a plaza that included a hole-in-the-wall club for the old heads, a pawn shop, and a big barbecue pit in the parking lot that used to service patrons of all of the above. That place was named Roger's Barber Shop. The owner, unsurprisingly named Roger, looked like he used to be in a soul group that opened for the Chi-Lites. He never cut me. I went to Ron, another one of my dad's friends. After a few years, Ron moved to another barbershop less than five minutes away from the old location. I can't recall the name of that shop, but I do remember that Ron used to wear eyeglasses that suggested he really missed the Run-DMC era. Once, Ron cut three parts in my hair, and I temporarily hated him for it. I used to keep a part in the front, but I didn't care for that degree of excessiveness. I felt that the money he was owed for that cut should have been spent instead in the McDonald's right across the railroad tracks (RIP to that long-demolished location) on a twenty-piece nugget and extra-large order of French fries as a reward for the emotional abuse I had just endured over superfluous cuts on the side of my head that I did not ask for. That barbershop closed abruptly, and I never knew where the hell Ron went after that. Maybe it was divine intervention, because who was to say he wouldn't have kept putting unrequested parts on the side of my head?

As I sought a replacement barber, my friend Kim introduced me to her brother Gary, who cut my hair at her mom's house. Gary was both an amazing barber and someone amazing to look at. However, despite not knowing what the word "patriarchal" meant at the time, I certainly knew how to frown whenever I heard a man drown me in machismo and casual sexism. Even so, though I didn't want to hear a lot of the things he had to say about women, I shrugged it off, because as much as he liked to talk, I liked to look at him while he expertly cut my hair. But, like Ron, he upped and disappeared, leaving my hairline once again in a state of total abandonment.

Kim then recommended I go see someone named Jaison. I loved Jaison because he had a sleeve of arm tattoos that went from his shoulder to his wrist and a quintessential Houston accent, and he read *Esquire*. In other words, he was the perfect mix of man. Moreover, as talkative as I could be, I could also sit in silence for long periods of time. Jaison never tried to force a conversation. If anything, I would push him for small talk, and, thankfully, he never made me regret it. Above all, Jaison cut hair like an artist, and I always left his chair feeling my most confident. For someone still dealing with weight issues and the occasional taunt about how slanted my eyes were or how big my two front teeth were, those moments of confidence proved vital.

Up until college, despite only a few unwanted parts here and there, my experiences with barbershops were mostly fine. That didn't mean I necessarily loved the waiting part before a cut, during which I had to be subjected to whatever conversation the men in the room were having. I was not a sports fanatic, but I was competent enough to tolerate those conversations. When it came to politics, even as a teenager, I found myself resisting the urge to correct the much older men who didn't have the slightest clue as to what they were talking about. Then there was the chatter about women, which often had me burying my head in a magazine or aggressively staring into the TV and pretending my senses were strong enough to make out what was being said over the loudness of everyone else.

And of course, every so often, I would hear homophobic comments made by men in the barbershop. For many gay Black men, the hypermasculine, ultrastraight spaces of the majority of Black barbershops were intimidating because they were so wildly unwelcoming. Even while fighting to admit the truth about myself, deep down, I knew much of their musings was intended to make people like me feel less-than. I had already been trained on how to ignore things I didn't want to hear due to the chaos in my own home. That's not to say I didn't wince at some points, but I had never been especially bothered until one particular visit.

It was my final year of college, so by then, I was already out and becoming more familiar with the art of brushing aside opinions about homosexuality that repulsed me. I went to see my regular barber at the shop located across the street from campus. One of the other barbers started a rant about gay clientele and how they behaved while in the chair. In his deluded mind, gay men wanted every single man around—including his bugawolf, few-clients-having ass.

"You know how those faggots get in the chair. They stick their elbows out, hoping to brush across your dick and shit. Punk-ass niggas."

His vitriol was met with laughter from much of the room. Everyone—including my barber—joined in on the "jokes." My barber in particular yukked it up, extending his elbows and doing what he felt were gay mannerisms to the delight of this other barber's stupidity and delusions of grandeur. That barber wouldn't stop his diatribe, going on to add that gay men needed to be rounded up and sent to a women's prison to be raped. In his mind, that was his way of curing an egregious perversion. He was one of those types who felt homosexuality was a conspiracy concocted by the white man to emasculate the Black man. By then, I had already taken a course on gender roles and relations. It was in that class—taught by a professor who looked exactly like my late grandmother—that I learned how most of our ideas of gender and sexuality stemmed from Western mores and customs that we traditionally had never embraced until they were forced on us through enslavement. I learned a lot about non-European cultures that didn't subscribe to gender binaries in the ways most of us have been conditioned into believing. Above all, I was informed that if not for the imperialistic, Bible-toting, and dogma-bastardizing white men who swooped in and forced their rigid nonsense on us through colonialism, maybe, just maybe, this man wouldn't have sounded so damn foolish in the barbershop.

Yet though I had knowledge of all of these things, I didn't put up a fight upon hearing this. In that moment, my silence allowed his ignorance to win. It wasn't that I didn't think to say anything. I wanted to, but I didn't want to bother anyone. It wasn't as if I was going to change any of their minds. Anyone who thought that of gay folks would not suddenly alter their point of view simply due to my standing in front of them. Life was not an after-school special. If anything, words would have been exchanged, and that scene could have easily ended up as a story on the evening news.

This just in: twenty-two-year-old Black Howard student stabs area barber to the white meat for talking out of turn about the gays with his bitch ass.

Meanwhile, as all of this was happening, I only had half of my head cut. You could literally see half my head trimmed down, and the other side still in the shape I walked in with. Cursing out someone with trimmers in his hand whose job was to give me a haircut didn't come across as the smartest move to make. So I let them win for the sake of my vanity and lack of faith in my anger-management skills.

After finishing up, I walked up to the East Towers, the dorm I lived in, and called Jordan, to whom I talked every so often. As I was describing everything that had happened, I broke into tears. I knew that man was ignorant and wrong. I knew I wasn't the person he was describing. I bawled anyway. I bawled because, while I was out, I hadn't been out that long. While I wouldn't describe Howard University as overwhelmingly welcoming to gay people at that time, I at least knew how to take care of myself in that environment. But just going across the street reminded me that there was an entire world out there, and a lot of it still didn't support my kind—even if we shared the same skin color. Mostly, I bawled because I was so goddamn angry and felt powerless.

While sobbing, I asked Jordan, "Is this going to be the rest of my life?" I'm not sure why I even asked him. He wasn't out. He was still trying to sort himself out. I got off the phone not long after that. Once I got those tears out of my system, I had effectively shaken off what had bothered me. I never again allowed myself to be as bothered by anything in the barbershop as I was that day. Note "as bothered," which doesn't mean I was cured but rather that I made a conscious choice to never allow someone else's prejudices to stun me to that extent again. It's not like a magical old white woman came to me and told me "Bibbidi-Bobbidi-Boo" and made me miraculously immune to anyone's ignorance. Homophobia remained horrific, but as far as my experiences in the barbershop went, I was able to prioritize my grievances. Part of my ability to disassociate myself so swiftly was partially rooted in my not being as easily clocked as other queer men. Not everyone could do that, and I did not pretend otherwise. For me, it remained a defining choice in my life, because while my barber was wrong for laughing at a homophobe claiming all gay men needed to be raped at a women's prison, there was another problem: he wasn't that damn good a barber to begin with.

He would always cut against the grain, meaning instead of cutting my hair in the direction it was trained to grow—i.e., my wave pattern—he went the opposite way, leaving me waveless. Now, it was my own fault for sticking by him. For a while, I stopped going to him and ended up walking around campus with a big afro that made me look as though I were auditioning to play Huey Freeman in the nonanimated version of *The Boondocks*. As a matter of fact, it wasn't long before I ended up back in his chair. And why? Because I was too lazy to go out and explore another barbershop. I would like to think living in a pre-Yelp, social media world excuses me partially, but that would be a lie.

—

As vain as I can be, I don't always make the best decisions about my hair. In fact, there's a ditzy quality to me. I sometimes decide to do things on a whim solely based on natural curiosity. Say, *Oh, I wonder what happens if I put this in reverse?* What happens is you nearly crash your car. Or, *Hmm, she just said I can make that spot; can I?* No, you fool, and now your mom has that scratch in her car. There are moments along the lines of, *Ooh, I'm allergic to this, but maybe trying it now will be different.* The end result is a bitch needing Benadryl.

This recklessness and penchant for danger has had an impact on my hair too, which is why for a month, I walked around Los Angeles as a Black Mickey Mouse.

I had just moved to that Koreatown area of Los Angeles. I knew nothing. I had no car. I didn't have a group of friends there yet. What I did know, though, was that it had been more than a week since I had gotten a haircut and I couldn't bear the uneven line I saw in the mirror. While walking around the new neighborhood, I saw a barbershop. Mistake number one: I was not in a Black neighborhood, so why would I think they would know how to cut my hair? I did see a Hispanic man there, which made me wonder if he would at least know how to line me up. As I walked up to ask him, he immediately told me that he was getting off. Next to him was a Korean man who didn't speak any English yet motioned for me to come to him anyway. Mistake number two: I sat down in his chair. Mistake number three: I did not immediately get up upon realizing that I was going to let a Korean man who didn't speak English cut my Black-ass hair. He pointed to a poster of different haircut styles. Mistake number four to infinity: I didn't take this as the Lord telling me to get the hell out of that barbershop and just ask someone to take me to Crenshaw or Inglewood later in the week.

All this Korean barber kept saying to me was, "Cut, cut." I was saying no, I want you to line it up. I literally took my fingers and showed him what I wanted. He didn't get that right at all.

Again, I knew better. My hairline is, was, and forever shall be weird. I have a cowlick, so on one side of the front of my head, my hair has always been oddly thinner, to the point that the hair in that area would sometimes just stick up. Over the years, I have had many a barber say to me in befuddlement or annoyance, "Man, it took me longer to line you up than anything else." A barber who knows what he's doing would spot this trouble and delicately cut around the area accordingly. Well, when you don't know how to communicate with the person cutting your hair, you have no real means of making certain that they are careful. The result? On one side of my head, it looked as if someone had forgotten their ruler or any tool that could be used to measure something accurately and opted to use a gnawed-on Toblerone in its place. The line on that side seemed to be headed in two separate directions. On the other side it was straight, but what did it matter when both sides of my head appeared to be in an unholy war? As for the top of my head, not only did he just ram over my cowlick despite me requesting just a lineup but he also went over the other side of my hair, which up until that moment I hadn't realized was beginning to thin in the front too. So, you had a crooked line on one side, a decent-enough line on the other, and in the front, a dedication to Mickey Mouse. On top of it all, he took the line so far back that I could reach back and grab my ancestors out of slavery. I had no idea how to say "I ought to beat your ass" in Korean, but I truly regret not knowing how to convey my rage.

When I got home, I immediately took pictures to show people the horror film I had willfully participated in. My mom laughed like hell at me and my idiotic decision. Kim got her chuckles in too. I can't say that I fault either of them. One of my roommates tried to stifle her laughter but gave in, only to follow her chuckles by quipping that I should have told the man that I was Barack Obama and then maybe I would have gotten a better lineup. Instead, I had walked out of there as a tribute to Sherman Hemsley.

For once, I tried to tame my neurotic need for a weekly barber-shop visit in order to try to grow my hair back. I ended up finding another barbershop—one that Black folks populated. Upon enter-ing the shop, I spotted one dude in his chair eating a fish plate out of a big Styrofoam box. Obviously, I went with him. As I sat down, I immediately said, "Okay, so I let someone mess me up, right." In-stantaneously, he said, "I can tell, bro." That meant it was as bad as I had thought it was, and that my friends had been lying to me to be kind. In this instance, kindness was for suckers; they should have demanded that I go buy a hat. I don't remember anyone saying anything homophobic at that shop, but I do know that after a while I grew tired of the barber asking me if I could write a movie for him. I moved away from Los Angeles, and he sent a friend request on Facebook with a message I never opened.

Once I moved to New York, I had to search once again for a competent barber I could depend on to not have me look the fool. Worse, by the time I arrived, I had to deal with the realities that stress, some medication, and bad barbers who didn't take direction well had done to my hair. It was a lil' thinner on both sides, but the hair continued to grow—only slower than everywhere else.

Some people have listened to my complaints and suggested I go bald. Those people can fuck off for all eternity. I still have a lot of hair and a lot of fight left in me, and with God, Rogaine for Men, and Jamaican black castor oil, I am still in this. Besides, so long as you channel your Ralph Tresvant and exercise some sensitivity on cutting my hair in the front, we gon' be alright.

The first barber I found in Harlem was identical to No Malice from the Clipse. This shop was on Frederick Douglass, and they had a dog there the size of the Camry I had left back in Texas. He cut my hair all right, but he required too many AMBER Alerts to schedule an appointment, so I ditched him. There was a lesbian in the shop that I thought to try, but she left. I later found out that it was because the men in the shop were a bit hostile toward her clientele. As in, all those gay boys. I didn't bother trying anyone else in that shop for that reason alone. I started trying out yet more barbers in the area, and each one was more terrible than the last.

Finally, I found D, who looked at my hair, sized up my issues without me even telling him, and told me, "I got you." It was the first time in years I had really been complimented about my cuts. The suggestion to switch to bald fades worked for me, but D kept pressing me to get a Bigen. A Bigen is a semipermanent hair dye activated by water with progressive product names such as "Oriental Black." Every week, D would swear getting a Bigen would settle my insecurities and make me look better. Anytime I'd seen someone with a Bigen, they looked cartoonish. I wouldn't let him do that to me. Had I not suffered enough from barbers over the years? Apparently not, because I went from "That's a nice fade" to "Who did that to you? Should I call the police?" He had the lines on the side of my head damn near kissing my earlobes. The first time he did it, he apologized and said he'd be more careful. A few weeks later, he fell back on old habits. Of course, this was around the same time he started to complain all the time about being a barber and how much he hated his job. No wonder I started walking around with a forehead far larger than I had ever known it to be.

At that point, the only thing that didn't bother me about D was that he never asked me about my sexuality. I imagine he knew, but thankfully he avoided a topic I didn't want to engage with him on.

He did talk about his women problems to me. All 99,000 of them that essentially amounted to the fact that he had a bit of a wayward dick, and the women he dealt with had issues about it. His shop ended up closing because of the rent increases in New York. I had no idea where D went, but by that time I wanted another barber anyway. He had become too hard to locate on any given day, and while I knew he was a good barber, those few cuts that played with my hairline once again triggered all the self-consciousness I had about getting older and the possibility that my hair might be thinning out to the point that I could no longer present myself the way I wanted to. Again, I'm not shaving my head. Quit telling me to do this. My peanut head is not made for that.

I found my most recent, and by far best, barber since leaving Houston on a whim and in a desperate search to look semidecent before an audition for an on-camera role on a TV show. It was an incredibly early Tuesday morning in January, and he was standing outside of Big Russ Barbershop looking cold. I asked if he could give me a lineup, and as I sat in the chair, I explained what every barber did wrong to my head and what not to do. After seeing how well he took direction, I went ahead and asked for him to give me a full cut. He introduced himself as Kalid and gave me his card, telling me I should come back since I liked the cut so much. So I did. After a while, I noticed that the barbershop was inclusive in both its clientele and its barbers.

Until this shop, I had never directly mentioned my sexuality, opting instead to hide in plain sight. Mostly because if I had once again been met with homophobia, I wasn't sure of how I would react. The silence that happened a decade prior was no longer going to happen should I be met with that sort of antagonism. I had the sneaking suspicion that if I did confirm that part about me, I wouldn't be made to feel uncomfortable. So much so that when the barber who cut directly in front of Kalid once engaged me in an ongoing conversation about having sex without condoms, I mentioned that I was gay and had long been paranoid about HIV/AIDS, so I'd never had condom-less sex. His mind wasn't blown because I said I was gay; he was mystified that I had that level of discipline. Then he told me, "I really hope you get to fuck someone without a condom. It's the best."

That's probably the kindest thing anyone has ever said to me inside of a barbershop. For the first time ever, this shop allowed me a glimpse into how straight Black men in the shop felt. For them, this was a place of community, or even therapy. For them, the conversations that happened informed their point of view.

There are plenty of straight Black men who have said to me that the barbershop is partially where they learned how to be a Black man in this world. I understand that, but as a Black man in this world who happens to be gay, my past experiences will never allow me to share their sentiments. I can never allow myself to feel completely comfortable in those spaces, because one, I've had way too many experiences with bad barbers, and two, I've never found those spaces to be welcoming to the sort of man that I am. While I do hope that the younger queer Black men who now go into those shops will never have to witness the sort of condemnations I did in years past, my expectations are extremely limited.

Now I go in there longing to shake off the sluggish feeling of my untamed mane and go back out into the world with the image I prefer to project. I do not go in there to be affirmed. I do not go in there seeking camaraderie. I do not need that place to be my sanctuary, because I've found mine elsewhere. Ideally, I hope those barber-shops become more welcoming to men who are not straight, but it is not a need that I personally have. I enter the space only with the determination to leave feeling beautiful. I know how this world views me as a Black person, as a Black man, as a gay man, as a Black gay man. I'm more than familiar with the hatred fuming on the outside. I am keenly aware of how some of those who look like me view me as beneath them. I wake up every morning having to face them all.

I just want to look my best each week when I do.

Several months later, I ran into D on the street, right after Kalid gave me a cut. D was on the phone, but told whoever he was talking to, "Let me call you right back." He asked where I'd been, as if I'd ditched him. I explained that I lost his number. Yes, that sounds like a lie, but I actually did, and, word to the wise, never forget the password to your Apple ID and break your phone in the same week. While he complimented my fade, he trashed the lineup and said I needed to come back and see him at the shop a few feet away from us. I didn't really plan to until I went home and looked more deeply into my hair. He was right. I went back to him the following week.

Pray for my hair.

Itchy and Scratchy

"**Y**our dick is dry," Chris declared in an exquisitely executed matter-of-fact fashion. He was not wrong. It had been at least two years since I had had sex. Still, the bitch could have been more sensitive. (Counterpoint: sensitivity is for Ralph Tresvant and people who can't always handle the truth.) I was in obvious need of at least three tablespoons of truth serum, and Chris proved willing and able to serve me some.

And so he did, over discounted well brown liquor at an East Village dive bar. I had moved and settled into life in New York, but true to form, my focus was much more on getting settled, making money (freelancers are always worried about making money, because you never know when a contract will be cut or some editor who just a week ago said you were everything mentions the words "budget slashed"), and working toward a future that didn't include me essay-hustling so much as getting laid. I had squandered my twenties by not having enough sex. If I were to rate my sex life in that decade through emojis now, I behaved like the yellow one with his eyes closed and a straight line where a smile should be. I should have acted more like a cross between the eggplant and the one nobody I know uses to signify actual raindrops. I had had plenty of ho moments, to be sure, but inconsistency over ten years riddled with the guilt that came with religious indoctrination and lingering insecurities had been the norm. Insert here that emoji that looks like someone gasping for air in utter agony.

I told myself that my thirties would be different. In fact, I wrote a whole essay about it. Rest in peace to *xoJane* and its series of "It Happened to Me" essays. I never got to write one of those, but when the remarkable Rebecca Carroll was editing the site, I did pen a piece about my struggles with intimacy, the source of that anxiety, and my resolution to letting go of past trauma and inhibitions and starting to have sex without all the emotional baggage I had been carrying. After my piece was published, strangers online were encouraging in a "You go, boy—don't press eject on your erections anymore!" sort of way. I also ended up talking about the piece on NPR with *the* Michel Martin. Michel Martin is so brilliant and so classy, which meant I spoke about the matter—in a *Tell Me More* segment entitled "Black, Gay, and Scared of Sex"—in as similar a manner as possible. I didn't master the talk-radio voice, but I did manage to avoid being crass and saying something like "Sis, I gotta quit bullshitting and get to the nuts." Gold star for me.

But I could talk about my sex life with Chris like that. My bluntness gave way to an even more direct reaction from him. He was pointed in his critique—telling me that I should learn to carve out a little more personal time to bust a nut because it was healthy to have sex. It was also becoming a bit obvious that I needed something to lower my rising stress levels, which were sooner or later going to lead me to spontaneously combusting. He advised me to "be a better gay" and have sex without having to engage in the getting-to-know-you process.

He had a suggestion on how to accomplish such a feat: going on "the apps." I admittedly rolled my eyes when he said it. Hookup apps like Jack'd and Grindr were an acquired taste, and for the longest time, I had no interest in acquiring that taste. Some people loathe these sorts of apps for "ruining romance" and contributing to the decline of the art of conversation.

So, about this: I too like the idea of two people meeting, connecting on some emotional-spiritual-whatever-phrasing-constitutes deeper-connection level, and going on to have amazing sex. To me, that gives way to the sort of fucking that leads to "Good lovin', body rockin', knockin' boots all night long, yeah / Makin' love until we tire to the break of dawn." But as I was learning with my sandy penis, there are also times that call for sex more along the lines of "Only ring your celly when I'm feeling lonely / When it's all over, please get up and leave." I made peace with that, but I wasn't sure if attaining the latter through an app was my kind of thing. I didn't think of myself as pure, but partaking in the apps, which screamed Seamless for Sex, felt degrading.

Then I had to check myself. Would using an app to have sex be all that different from the years I had spent on instant messenger and the direct-message sections of various message boards? What *had* I been doing on instant messenger and the direct-message sections of various message boards? Being a junior-varsity cyber-slut-ass ho, that's what! Back when I had peak fear of intimacy and dying from complications related to some incurable sexually transmitted disease, I did some questionable things, depending on what God you serve and dogma you adhere to. Those would include doing virtual peep shows for people on camera as michael02808 with a Logitech camera purchased from Best Buy. Nothing was ever recorded—or at least I don't think it was. (I guess I'll find out when I launch my senatorial campaign sometime in my sixth decade of life.) As much shame as I felt each and every time I engaged in virtual ho shit, overall, I can't say that I regret any of it. In a lot of ways, it helped me. It gave me validation as a sexually desirable being. If I could see the benefit of engaging in sexual voyeurism with a gleeful half-Black boy living in Amsterdam and bonding over our similar taste in nineties and early-aughts R & B acts, why not see the benefits of apps? If AOL and Yahoo Messenger had functioned as my virtual whoring, weren't the apps just thotting in 3-D?

The more I thought about it, the more my hesitation waned, and I eventually had a change of heart. It took a minute for me to truly engage with these apps, however. Initially, I would log on and promptly punk out with the underlying concern that motherfuckers were crazy out there. Ultimately, I fully gave in and signed up for Jack'd, which was described as a "gay men's social network." (Okay, sure.)

It was a rocky experience for me from the jump. The first person that came over just performed fine work with his mouth and was promptly sent on his way. Once he finished and exited, I couldn't find my keys. I sprinted to my paranoia and was certain that he had stolen my keys and was planning to return to my apartment to slit my throat. Hours went by, and I cursed the state of New York for not having loose gun laws like Texas did. Naturally, this was happening the day before New Year's Eve—meaning my super was off for the next couple of days. As for calling a locksmith, well, there were two doors you had to go through in order to get into my building so me changing, the locks on both was not an option.

At the time, I didn't know many of my neighbors. The dude who kept saying, "Well, when you and the white people moved in," to my immediate objection ("My nigga, I would be living in Harlem regardless, so don't lump me in with folks who discovered Harlem four minutes ago after reading about just how lovely it is "now" in the *New York Times*). The Black woman who looked like the older second cousin of Maxine Shaw from *Living Single*. The unfriendly white gay dude who lived in the unit between us. And that louder woman downstairs who remembered my name, though I could never remember hers (I just called her "Drunk Millie Jackson" in my mind). She was particularly unreliable. She was always banging on my window to let her in all the time. She constantly woke me up arguing with her man, whom she swore she was over but who never left. Whenever he put her out or she lost her keys in between her eighth glass of E&J and third Marlboro of the evening, she would bug me to let her in. "I'm so sorry, Michael." A lie.

None of these people seemed to be home. So, for hours I contemplated my new life as that fool who had trapped himself in his apartment for days because he was horny and allowed some man to show him exactly "what dat mouf do." Some writers can be hermits who lock themselves in their places of residence for days at a time. I'm not that person, but even if I were, that should only be an option rather than a scenario forced upon you.

After all of this drama, I ended up finding my keys in one of my kitchen cabinets while I was trying to locate a pan to bake the chicken nuggets I planned to have for emotional eating purposes.

What actually made me feel the fool about all of this was that

this guy turned out to be best friends with a man I would spot several months later and immediately fall for. This man was gorgeous,
smart, incredibly talented, creative, kind, and, of course, from
Louisiana—a southern experience I could easily relate to. God rest
my stunning grandma's soul, but he was the sort of man that even
if she had a problem with her grandson's being gay, she would have
looked at this man and said, "Well, if you're gonna be a homo, this
is the way to do it." It was too all-perfect, which is exactly why I
screwed it up from the very beginning. Of course, when we eventually hung out, he didn't mention that his bestie had told him much
more than, "We went on a date once." In fact, he had told him everything, because as that guy had already proven, it was hard for him
to close his mouth. Fuck him forever for being a hater and not allowing me the chance to scare his friend away on my own terms!

There were other problems too. Although I was using the screen
name "Slim Shady" on Jack'd, the anonymity often afforded to users
wasn't going so well for me. I was getting messages like: "Hey, Michael. I love your blog, The Cynical Ones! You've been such an inspiration to me." Then I started being asked if was "@youngsinick from
Twitter," and again came conversations about my work as a writer.
It hadn't dawned on me that to some—namely, those younger than
me or around the same age I was, who largely populated this app—I
was one of the few working gay Black male writers they might know
of. When I shared this with my friend Alex, he said, "I don't get how
you feel like you wouldn't get recognized. You're an openly gay jour-
nalist who writes everything, everywhere. All these Negroes aren't
illiterate, ignorant bottoms." Fair. On the one hand, it was flattering
to be recognized and to be complimented on my work. Having said
that, this wasn't really the point of my being on the app. To this day,

I've yet to get hard over someone complimenting me on one of my essays.

Not to mention, while I had gotten over my own stigma against "the apps," the same could not be said of others. I worried that being clocked would lead to people drawing certain conclusions about me, that they would judge me. Soon, someone I was interested in said that someone else had screencapped a conversation of mine from Jack'd and posted it in some Facebook group. I didn't know what the group was for; it was probably for bitches that couldn't mind their own business. I never asked what people were saying about my conversation. I just immediately deleted the app.

A month later I reinstalled it, then days later deleted it again. I repeated that cycle for a while—as so many of us do. In between deleting after masturbating or reinstalling when that wasn't enough, there did end up being one person who was more than just a one-off. I didn't know his name. I never cared to learn it. He never knew mine, which was what I had intended. He came over for one reason, and when we finished, I sent him on his way. For the sake of following along, I'll call him "Itchy."

In the summer of 2015, I had a bedbug scare. Before moving to New York City, I didn't know a solitary thing about bedbugs. Upon moving here, I learned that bedbugs were some sort of real-life monsters under your bed only far worse, because these demonic beasts could attack every inch of your mattress and various parts of your body. Guess who woke up one damn day in July with huge red bumps on his left leg and the top areas of his back? The bumps on my knees and lower leg were as big as the head of that star of the cartoon series *Bobby's World*. As in big as fuck. There were also bites from my knee down to my ankle. I immediately took pictures and sent them to my mama, whom I consult for every medical emergency. She didn't know what the hell was on my leg and back. She thought maybe it was some sort of spider. Then it hit her and me at the same damn time: *Are these the damn bites of those disgusting-ass bugs?!*

I saw no signs of them anywhere, so it was difficult to prove. I did drop an email to my landlord about it. He sent the super, who checked out my apartment—specifically the bed—and saw no signs of the pests. He came back with one of those bug bombs. I had read about those sorts of contraptions and how they didn't work on bedbugs at all. So he dropped that lil' bomb on me and had me out of my place for hours to fix a problem with the wrong equipment. What could go wrong?

Two weeks went by, and I ended up not having any more bite marks. Not long after, I saw more bites in a similar pattern on my left leg, as well as on the top of my right arm. Frantic, I threw out a ton of things in my apartment—the bedspread, the sheets, the pillowcases—and a ton of clothes. The clothes I did keep, I went down the street and tossed them in the dryer to kill whatever bugs may have gotten on them, and then I stuffed them into multiple garbage bags. I also enclosed my mattress in one of those weird plastic things that's supposed to keep bedbugs out. Most of this was semi-reasonable, but I have a habit of behaving like a full-fledged fool when frantic. I couldn't get over the sight of the hideous bumps on my skin, so I put toothpaste on them. Why would I be so dumb? Well, my logic was that toothpaste could get rid of pimples, so maybe they could get rid of these too. Yeah, I have three marks on my leg that are basically burning stains from that. As successful as the cocoa butter had been in returning my skin to its usual presentation after sitting on a fire-ant bed in Houston, I didn't have as much luck with it when it came to my decision to deal with this latest setback.

When I finally met with a dermatologist, she charged me way too much money to say that she couldn't confirm that the bites had come from bedbugs because in New York City, it could have been anything. She prescribed me a cream, but she could have saved me a co-pay and travel had she just filled my prescription when I called her.

A month and change went by, and there were no bites. I couldn't figure out the source of the problem. Was it the train? Was it the Magic Johnson Theater? Was it my gym? I had no idea until I let Itchy come through again. Sexual eruptions were not happening in the midst of this, so when Itchy came over, it was intended to be a much-needed release. The next morning, the bumps were back. That's when I realized: IT WAS THIS MAN.

I confided to my friend La, a person I loved but who was also someone who lived to troll me no matter the circumstance. I told her that I had been getting these bumps that could be from bedbugs, but since I had never found any, I could not know for certain. She went in. "Nigga! Are you fucking somebody with fleas?" It was via text, but I could feel her laughter through my iPhone. I didn't know where she had gotten fleabites from, but after quickly Googling to find out what fleabites looked like, I decided that may have been the case. I was beyond embarrassed. All I ever wanted was a release, and I ended up with a prescription, a torn-up apartment, and the loss of a lot of clothes that I couldn't even get a tax write-off for because I didn't want to be responsible for spreading the evil.

For the record, the dude didn't look dirty. I mean, he seemed like he smoked weed as much as I drank water, but there were plenty of squeaky-clean weedheads. Needless to say, I laid off the apps for a significant time. Once I did go back on—about a year later—guess who clocked me on Grindr? He wanted to come over, and what did I say? Have you bathed at least four times today? Have you burned every article of clothing you've owned within the past twelve years? Have you burned your place of residence down in the name of the antibug movement?

No, I didn't say any of that. I thought to simply block him and delete the app all over again and go catch up on the dozens of articles in my Pocket app that deservingly felt abandoned.

But in the end, I let him come over, but only to give me head. I tried to rationalize it all. I would pull my sheets away. I would spray the mattress down as soon as he left. I would turn on gospel music and pray for an hour that I didn't wake up once again being the Scratchy to his Itchy. Right before he came by, I knew how pathetic I was being. I was disgusted with myself. Still, I let him blow me anyway. It was not worth it. I put my balls at risk. What if whatever he had crawling on him had planned to finish me off by way of attacking one of my testicles and killed me? I looked in the mirror, stared deep into myself, and wondered aloud, "What in the fuck is wrong with you, Michael?" I was not protecting my sac or my spirit. I knew better, and it was time to act like it.

After that, I gracefully bowed out of regular usage of the apps. When I say "regular usage," I mean that between the final thirty-six hours of 2013 and early fall 2015, I would go on there every now and again for, uh, stuff. After that, I downloaded them whenever I wanted to be reminded of how awful men were. Then I joined Tinder, which was where you matched with attractive people to go on actual dates, although fun fact: most of the people you match with have no real interest in conversation, much less meeting in person. As fate would have it, I would later become a columnist at *Into*, a digital magazine for the modern queer world launched by Grindr. I never told the editor in chief, Zach Stafford, that I may or may not have been exposed to fleas in the past by using one of the apps and that I considered the column to be my reparations.

Despite somehow finding myself once again at the intersection of vengeful insects and fornication, I do like that I allowed myself the space to let go of certain hang-ups I held about the apps and applauded myself for not denying human instinct. But every now and then, I see the scars on my left leg and remember that I always have to be good to my balls. For they have always been so good to me.

My Lord and Gyrator

My father was a presence in my life (for better and for worse), but there were things no straight man, much less one like him, could teach a little boy who was into boys. The fishing trips were fun. I also liked swinging and kicking on the punching bag he pinned up in the garage for me and my little brother. I enjoyed all of the designated "boy" things he introduced me to, but he probably clocked other characteristics about me (only he dared not speak of them). And despite my undoubtedly being my mother's son in many ways, I could tell that she had similar blind spots. This is not a shot at them. They understood life as they had been raised to view it, and that vision did not extend to little boys with certain traits that may or may not have raised eyebrows. It was easier to cater to the more aggressive, traditionally masculine aspects of me than it was to those that came across as softer, feminine, "girly." It didn't help much that I wasn't able to get out and explore life in my teenage years in the way that many teens have the opportunity to do. My mother was strict, and there was only so much I could do—and, as a result, see and experience.

In such a state of confinement, I found pop culture to be a saving grace. For many who lack access financially, emotionally, physically, or some combination of the three, pop culture is how we get to access perspectives from outside our bubbles. It helps to inform us of who we are in our present, developing who we ultimately might become. The man I've become has largely been molded by the lessons learned from the famous women I've obsessed over throughout the course of my life.

My mother told me that she explained sex to me when I was three. Unsurprisingly, it was in the context of procreation. She reminded me of this fact ten years later, when I was thirteen. While walking to the refrigerator—probably to have my eleventh sausage sandwich—I made some quip in response to some talk show segment related to teenage pregnancies. I asked her when she had first told me about sex, and that's when she reminded me. It made sense to me, because I couldn't recall not ever knowing about sex, or at least how babies were made.

Now, when I was thirteen, my mom quickly followed up with how to put a condom on. I was like, "All right, now, Mama, I'm not having sex!" It wasn't so much that she encouraged me to have sex. In fact, her position was a staunch "Don't do it!" Still, she was a nurse who, for decades, primarily took care of new mothers—including incredibly young ones. Fortunately for her fears of becoming a grandmother far too soon, I was getting fat and developing a complex. There was also the whole thing where Kenneth in honors biology, not Kim, was looking appealing to me.

My mom's medical background provided a technical explanation of a specific kind of sex. As for my dad, we have never, ever talked about sex. He warned me repeatedly in my childhood to never get married, but when it came to talking about sex, not a single remark. Perhaps that was why, as most of my teachers from K–12 were women, I always looked to them as authorities, sources of information on how things were.

Having said that, neither my mother nor any other woman or man around me spoke about sex outside of the sentiment "Ho, don't do it" and lamentations about unplanned pregnancies and sexually transmitted diseases. And no one said anything outside the prism of vaginal sex. And absolutely no one spoke of sex in terms of pleasure. Around the same time my mom mentioned condoms, I went to a record store called Soundwaves to purchase T-Boz of TLC's first solo single, the promasturbation anthem "Touch Myself." According to the poster of the Ten Commandments that used to hang on the wall in the room I shared with my younger brother—a poster featuring a white man with graying hair and surprisingly good muscle definition—masturbation was adultery, and per that, adultery was in violation of the seventh commandment.

T-Boz had a solid counterargument: "I don't think it's wrong to touch yourself / Ain't nothing wrong with making it feel good!"

It did indeed feel good; thus the point went to T-Boz (and Debra Killings singing background vocals), with apologies to Moses. Then there was Lil' Kim, who rapped "I used to be scared of the dick, now I throw lips to the shit," on the iconic "Big Momma Thang." Granted, I was a wee bit late to fully embrace the lyric, but it spoke to me all the same. Listening to women talk about sex felt right, because we shared a similar interest in men. There was only so much you could glean from men singing about women in ways that, try as you might have, just didn't appeal to you. I loved the way Mr. Dalvin from Jodeci looked in the "Come and Talk to Me (Radio Remix)" and "Cry For You" videos, but I just wanted his clothes and wondered what he looked like underneath them. I can also say this about so many other singers and rappers. Kim, Trina, and Foxy Brown objectified men in ways that I could relate to; even openly gay male singers of that era (and our current one) largely ignored overt expressions of their desire. So, these women appealed to me, 'cause what else did I have? Furthermore, these women were ostracized for being so sexual. Their behavior was taboo—just like gay sex. So when it came to sex, my mother had taught me the mechanics, but female recording artists filled the gaps. That was the only real kind of sex ed I'd ever had.

As far as visible depictions and musings about homosexuality went, Janet Jackson and Madonna each informed me about sex, but also taught me much more than merely the act of sex. I didn't know anything about ball scenes from the eighties and nineties, but I did have a chance to see Black and Latino men in their element by way of "Vogue." I was far too young to understand the politics behind Madonna's tapping into that subculture for her art at the time, but I did know it was through Madonna that I saw my first images of nonwhite gay men that didn't come across as caricature. That *In Living Color* sketch "Men on . . ." in which Damon Wayans and David Alan Grier portray Blaine Edwards and Antoine Merriweather, respectively, scared me as a child. With Madonna, the men looked free; on that show, they looked like fools. The slightest semblance of femininity from a Black man warranted that degree of ridicule.

You don't forget that kind of idea when it's presented to you in such a direct, mocking way. Madonna offered a counterpoint, even if it was one I wouldn't lean on until I was older. Similarly, since I didn't have the language to properly challenge the religion in which I was raised, through Madonna—a recovering Catholic herself—I was at least introduced to the novel concept that it was reasonable to look at religion and challenge what you'd been told to believe. (My catechism teachers had no idea she was the culprit behind my many, many questions during CCE classes.)

Janet Jackson was probably the most impactful pop star of my K–12 years. In elementary school, I used to wear these green denim shorts—think pine, not lime, emerald, or feces green—and in homage to her, I would wear their top button undone. Sometimes, hateful teachers would demand that I button myself all the way up. My love for Janet's background dancer Omar Lopez is well known among my close friends. But when I think about albums like *The Velvet Rope*, I remember a period during which she slapped me with so many heavy topics that I wasn't at all ready to handle but nonetheless needed to hear. I didn't know how to describe these sad feelings inside of me, but at least she provided a partial soundtrack to them. And her musings weren't confined to sex. She sang about domestic violence as I continued to remain silent about what I had witnessed in my own home.

Most people would assume that when I first heard "Free Xone," the closeted gay in me gleamed as a woman I practically worshipped sang out against homophobia. The same about "Together Again," a track dedicated to friends Janet had lost to AIDS. No and no. On the contrary, those songs freaked me the fuck out. I could listen to the DJ Premier remix of "Together Again" because the shit slapped, but I actively tried to ignore the messaging behind it. "Free Xone" boasted lyrics such as "Boy meets boy / Boy loses boy / Boy gets cute boy back," so I would skip that track and turn on "My Need." I would fantasize about boys and then feel guilty, fearing I was hellbound if I ever acted on those feelings.

All of these women introduced me to themes and affirming imagery and messaging early on; indeed, many of the lessons came before I had left high school. Still, I had yet to go out into the world and figure out my own place in it. Little by little, as I grew more comfortable with myself, the nuggets they had dropped were picked back up, and I found greater meaning in them.

Nevertheless, when I think about the last and most impactful pop-culture figure of my life, I think of my lord and gyrator: Beyoncé Giselle Knowles-Carter.

———

She is the beginning, end, and body roll to me. I have loved this woman from the very first Destiny's Child video. Long before you other folks banded together to launch the BeyHive, I was setting the stones for the building that housed our meetings with the other true believers. When I listen to Beyoncé, I hear home. Like me, she went to Welch Middle School, and probably heard boys and girls doing the same slow, hazy kind of flow heard on songs such as Lil' KeKe's "Pimp Tha Pen" and Big Moe's "Barre Baby" during lunch in the cafeteria. I know Beyoncé is someone who listened to 97.9 the Box and heard the same New Orleans bounce mixes played throughout the day. I'm sure of it, because "Get Me Bodied" sounds like something by someone who grew up routinely hearing DJ Jubilee's "Get It Ready" and loved it so much that she wanted to create something that would both pay homage and offer her own spin on it. When

Beyoncé does her choreography, she reminds me of the same majorettes I saw at Madison High School, Yates High School, and Willowridge High School football games. That's why she is always on beat—because majorettes never, ever miss a beat.

I love that she has remained country as hell and country in a way that is very specific to a Black girl born in Houston but with Louisiana roots. I love that when R & B began to decline on radio, she never picked up a glow stick and joined the EDM wave like so many others fighting to stay relevant. Obviously, she made this choice long after she had cemented her place in music and culture, but there's still something admirable about a Black woman forgoing trends that pander to white people at the expense of Black creativity. As a Black creative, I know all too well what it's like to be urged to tone down who you are, sold under the pretense that it broadens your appeal to the "mainstream." I didn't have to wait for the *Beyoncé* and *Lemonade* albums to know Beyoncé was pro-Black, because choosing to stand firm in who you are and the culture that shaped you is a testament to caring about Blackness, Black culture, and Black people. As a writer who has existed in mainstream media and Black media alike, I know how much more the former means to many people than the latter, regardless of their race or ethnicity, so even if only on a symbolic level, Beyoncé's stance on remaining exactly as she's always been no matter what is happening around her has instilled in me the strength to remain the Gulf Coast ratchet bird I am.

Yet when I think about what Beyoncé most means to me, I think of my friend once saying, "You dance like a faggot." Jeanne, a lesbian and a dear friend, once shouted it out from the back seat of my car as I danced perhaps far too aggressively while driving to the club. She meant it as a compliment—which she quickly noted after seeing the visible discomfort on my face. For an extremely long time, I didn't dance publicly because it was one of the characteristics that I always felt was a dead giveaway about my queerness. I never wanted to be perceived like Blaine Edwards and Antoine Merriweather or any of the other gay men in various films and television shows who played similar depictions of the effeminate gay Black man whose only real duty was to service those who want to laugh at a sissy. I remember my mom driving me home from school once, and out of the blue remarking, "Some people probably mock the way you walk and the way you talk." At the time, that had not yet started to happen, but by the time I entered middle school, it was indeed an issue. Sometimes I took the insults in stride; other times I swung on their asses. It depended on the question of how much I wanted to let it get to me. The answer depended on my mood, and my mood was typically shaped by the degree of madness coming from father at my home.

As for how I walk . . . I haven't the slightest idea. I don't know. I've never organized a focus group or had someone record me in motion for analysis. I don't think I walk with a twist. I don't think I strut. Honestly, I have flat, skinny feet, and unless I'm wearing a pair of tennis shoes—pardon my country, *sneakerheads*—that fit just right, my feet normally hurt, and that's largely been my only focus when I walk. When it comes to how I talk, that too is subjective. For the most part, I speak in a monotonous tone. As a Houstonian, many of us, much like Beyoncé, speak with a slower cadence. Louisiana is a few hours away; both sides of my family are rooted there and some, depending on where they are from, can talk at much faster speeds. My dad is from a teensy town in Texas, but he speaks with the speed of a category-five hurricane. The more engaged I am—or, as I've learned since the age of twenty-one—the drunker I am, the faster I talk and my voice goes a lot higher. In my final year of college, I had to take a NewsVision course to complete my degree in broadcast journalism. That included me planning and shooting my own segments to be presented for the class. I remember the reaction to the first three I had to do: no one besides the two stunts from New Orleans could make out what I was saying. I spoke fast and high and befuddled the rest of the folks in the course. It was so bad that Professor Lewis, who liked me but wanted me to be coherent, offered a tip: "Tap your feet and speak with the pace of those slower taps, Speedy Gonzalez." This helped a bit, but I also tended to speak with my hands—a trait that read as feminine.

I used to hate the sound of my voice. And I used to hate watching video of me, seeing how I performed all these actions that registered as "gay." That's why, as much as I enjoyed tracks like "Vogue," I certainly didn't dance to them in public. In fact, I didn't dance in public at all.

That was why, when Jeanne said that I danced "like a faggot," I paused for a second. It was something I needed to get over, and learning to shake off that stigma came with a soundtrack: Beyoncé's majorly up-tempo and entirely glorious 2006 album, *B'Day*.

One of my favorite videos from the pre-visual album era was for "Freakum Dress." I loved how much that video recalled Vanity 6 and Apollonia 6—groups I had learned of by way of my big sister. As in the old Madonna videos and tours, there were gay Black men acting completely and utterly femme—and completely comfortable with that femininity. So, when I started hearing "Freakum Dress" in the club—or, hell, while walking on a sidewalk—I stopped fighting the urge not to react in public the way I did in private. The same went for the bonus tracks on the album like "Back Up" and "Lost Yo Mind," which gay Black clubs played obsessively in cities such as Houston, New York, Washington, DC, and Atlanta.

When *Dangerously in Love* came out, I used to do the choreography to "Baby Boy" in the oversized dorm room I had my sophomore year of college. It was a shame I didn't do it in public where it counted. Let's be clear that I'm not really coordinated enough to perform full-out choreography. I'll say that it's not impossible, but it would take me too long to learn the steps, because my attention span blows with the wind and I'd rather just dance like a free-spirited thot. Aliyah, my very first friend at Howard, once told me at Club Love in DC (RIP) during our junior year—after I was out and ready to twerk—"Yo, Mike, you dance like a stripper and the rent is due." God, what a sweet soul she is. I keep it in my back pocket whenever I need to pull out a pick-me-up in this awful world we live in. Naturally, when Aliyah said this, I was dancing to Beyoncé. I don't dance like that as much anymore because I'm getting older and worry about my knees, but every now and then, I remember to stretch and prove I still have it in me. Some of this comes from inner strength, but obviously that inner strength was instilled in me by Our Lady of Creole Goodness, Beyoncé. Ugh. I love her so much.

———

I actually met Beyoncé once in 2011 in Los Angeles, which was the site of that year's NBA All-Star Game. It was at some CAA party that I was able to go to as a plus-one of my friend Candy. It had been a long time coming. When I was an intern at the radio station in Houston in 2003, no one had told me Beyoncé was going to be there and that I could have come to fall on my knees and honor my savior. I only knew it was happening because while en route to mass on a Saturday evening, I got a text like, "Why aren't you here?" *BE-CAUSE NONE OF YOU SELFISH JACKASSES TOLD ME. THAT'S WHY. FUCK. FUCK. FUCK. FUCK.* No, I will never forgive them. We could have met that day and bonded over a shared love of Pappadeaux's and fried alligator. She could have gotten so smitten with me that she would have just told me to get in the car with her team and make a living carrying her purse. I would have said, "Hell yes, Miss Massa!"

Eight years later, I finally got to bow before the presence of greatness. It took a minute to get in. The fire marshall was being spiteful by putting our safety first and not allowing more people in. J. Cole was standing outside with the rest of us until he went around to another entrance for famous people who didn't care about the fire code. Eventually, we made our way inside. It was packed as hell, and as we were making our way through the crowd to find the free alcohol these rich people were providing, I heard Candy shout, "Michael, Beyoncé is coming this way!" I turned into the fastest sprinter on the planet and bypassed the lessers to make my way to glory. While rushing, I spotted Ryan Phillippe, who under any other circumstances would have warranted my full attention. But I had to walk on by his fine ass because I was on a mission.

Candy pointed in the direction of Beyoncé, and I rushed that way.

As soon as I spotted her, I did what any reasonable person would do: I started bowing. I couldn't do a complete drop because there were too many people. But I did the best I could to pay homage. I think she appreciated it. So, I tapped her and said, "I'm from Houston." Then she looked at me and smiled. "You from Houston?" I went, "Yeah and actually my brother went to Johnston with Solange. Same year." She touched me after and was like, "That's cool." She was not being fake about it either. Her smile and the way she raised her voice in response were genuine.

Then she smiled at me and touched my shoulder. Now, when Oprah had spoken at my college graduation, I had felt my credit score rising, but this was much more spiritual than that. I immediately felt like I was a better man. I asked for a hug, and she hugged me. She was leaving the party, so after the embrace, she floated away, and Candy just kept repeating "Oh, my God!"

I should note that Jay-Z was standing behind Beyoncé the whole time. As much as I love Jay-Z, I am a gay Black man from Houston, Texas, so my focus was on her, not him.

Hours after it happened, a friend of mine asked, "Did you act like a stan or did you act like a normal person?" What a ridiculous question. Of course I acted like a stan. If you don't act like a stan when you meet Beyoncé, something is wrong with you. I wasn't about to play it cool like she was the Pope or something. No, no, no, parts one and two.

By the way, the person who asked this was a Beytheist. A Beytheist is someone who denies the splendor of Beyoncé. I don't get people like that. I feel like they have a disability that's somehow contagious, which is why I've developed a rule to stop dating men who dislike Beyoncé. I have tried to respect other people's religious beliefs, but sometimes the biases you develop are well-earned. I've learned my lesson when it comes to Beytheists: they're garbage human beings who don't deserve to be around someone like me, a person with much better taste in music, a wiser embrace of excellence, and a champion of a Black woman who never let a beat bet her out. Can I get an uh oh, uh oh, uh oh, oh no no?

I wish I could have talked to Beyoncé longer, though. I wish I could have told her what an impact she's had on my life. How she motivates me with her work ethic. How her music brings the kind of joy that I can barely put into words. And, yes, how her femininity made me comfortable with the parts of me that read as feminine. And how I find that to be a source of strength, maybe even more than the other side, because masculinity is never put down the way femininity can be. It shouldn't have taken me so long to accept that side. The strongest people I know are my mother, my sister, and other women I've been fortunate enough to befriend along the way. So many women provided insight into my sexuality in my formative years, but even in my appreciation for them as complex, strong, phenomenal women, I made the mistake of not seeing their femininity as so vital an influence on me. Beyoncé was the one who helped me understand this, and in the end, she gave me the confidence to fully accept all parts of myself. These days, I like to describe myself as someone sitting at the intersection of Beyoncé and Bun B. She'll know what I mean. She's from Houston.

It's probably too late to become besties. If it's not, let the record show that I would happily sign whatever NDA is required to be around her. The same goes for human sacrifices.

I would like to think I will cross paths with her again. Ideally, it would be at Pappadeaux's at 610, the one closest to me and the one she used to always go to. We would sit over a lot of fried alligator and so many Swamp Things and I would tell her everything. And I would thank her, because if not for her and the other women I've admired over time, I wouldn't be this man I enjoy being now. I feel like she'd get that.

And if that never happens, I will continue to say thanks as I always do: by giving her whatever dollar amount she requires of me for great seats at her concerts—where I dance proudly, without fear or worry.

The Marrying Kind

If it were to ever happen, I have long had a working idea of how it would all go. After months of working out with an annoying but highly effective trainer I found on Instagram who I thought was sexy but turned out to be straight (I will try to respect his lifestyle choices), I will have achieved my goal in creating the sort of body I've always dreamed of having. I don't necessarily mean perfect IG thot physique, but I will no longer have the love handles with which I developed a codependent relationship back in my chubbier years. As a result of those lofty goals being met, he will find me standing in front of the mirror freakishly observing myself in a ridiculously expensive suit that I hopefully didn't pay for minutes before the ceremony is to begin. It fits perfectly. Yes, I am being self-involved, but in light of the event at hand, I'm well within my rights to stunt on you hoes. The selfies will soon commence, only to be interrupted by various friends joining together to screech, "Bitch, get over yourself. We need to start."

After their reality check is cashed, we all make our way to the ultrafancy room that I can now afford in my post-private-student-loan-debt world. We will not be at a church. God will be with us in spirit because God is omnipotent, but this won't go down at God's house. Maybe we'll be at the Museum of Fine Arts in Houston. Perhaps we will be at a garden—albeit a garden located somewhere in the country where it won't be unbearably hot or too damn cold. Extremes only work for me if I am ordering Popeyes following a long night of drinking or a good ole time with some weed.

Before I make my way down the aisle, there will be a shot waiting for me at the door, as my nerves will be bad. Plus, why not have one? It's a party, after all. Someone will then quickly cue the DJ, and my march, which is more like a subtle strut, will begin. The song blaring from the speakers is Beyoncé's "Get Me Bodied." My march that's more like a strut soon shifts to a jig. I'm dancing all up and down the aisle, and not long after the wedding attendees rise from their seats at the appropriate time—the call-and-response portion of the extended mix, obviously—proceed to drop down low and sweep the flo' with it. Preferably, Beyoncé is there in person. Like, we should be besties by then. If not, she will at least be there in spirit because I carry her with me wherever I go. Duh.

I'm not doing that gendered nonsense where one groom does the bride part and the other groom is the manly man. The other groom will get his moment down the aisle too. Just my luck he'll pick some song I hate like "Thong Song" or "One Sweet Day," but since I love him, whatever. Have your moment, dude.

(I'm totally kidding.)

(I would never marry anyone who still listens to "Thong Song." At best, he can get away with SisQó's "Got to Get It.")

The reception will be catered by the No Limit gold-selling female rapper and legend Mia X, who has since started cooking. She will do double duty with a performance of "Party Don't Stop." My husband and I will fill in for Foxy Brown and Master P. (Master P will probably charge too much, and while I adore Fox Boogie, she is an insurance risk. She once performed at a New York Black Pride event and fell off the stage. I don't have the time to worry about rap royalty tripping over their 37,000-inch weave on my watch.) The reception will be an all-night party. I'm not cheap, so the bar will be open, though I might require that the alcohol be served in either a champagne flute or a red Solo cup. The combination is me in a nutshell: country as hell, but into nice things when I can afford them. For those who require an emotional roller coaster at a wedding, I'll definitely include cry-inducing songs. Once all that wraps, we'll go to whatever island that won't be in some ferocious hurricane's path that summer. Scratch that: we're going somewhere inland with a pool. He'll deal. I can't swim anyway.

The only other wedding option I have since thought of goes like this: I wake up early one Sunday morning, bop my man on the head in bed, and say, "Yo, we really need to get this arrangement on paper. What if my clumsy ass falls down somewhere, breaks a leg, and finds out I have some kind of rare disease and your ass can't see me in the hospital?" And then we run down to the courthouse or whatever. Maybe get some Chick-fil-A afterward for irony's sake. That's equally romantic . . . and cheaper.

———

Most of the conversations that I have about marriage are with straight people. And whenever the subject of marriage comes up with the straights, I am either going along with the conversation for the sake of not playing spoiler or assuring my friends that no matter what article is floating across social media, there is still hope that they will get married and put some buns that oven. In truth, though, as optimistic as I can be for others about the subject, I have long maintained ambivalence toward the institution of marriage. For most of my life, I did not have to tackle those mixed feelings. I could put them on the sidelines and let them fester, because it was not as if the freedom to marry a man was a nationwide right. Little by little did that start to change, depending on the state, and as the marriage-equality wave spread, I eventually had a seat directly in front of the possibilities.

In 2014, I attended a gay wedding. Derrence, whom I knew from high school, was marrying Nick Denton, whom I didn't know personally but who I certainly recognized as the founder of Gawker. Their wedding was at the American Museum of Natural History in New York. It was both the first time I saw two dudes tie the knot and the first time I had seen more than two people from high school outside of Houston—the latter of which was the more surprising aspect of the day. It was also my first fancy wedding, as evidenced by the fact that it was covered by the *New York Times*. If you want to feel poor, attend a One Percent wedding.

Like me, Derrence had a strong affinity for Queen Bey, which was why I heard a pianist play the instrumental of "Dangerously in Love" so much throughout the ceremony. I came with dré. It was a black-tie affair, so I had ended up buying a tuxedo, assuming that if I worked in media and lived in New York City, I'd presumably be required to wear one every so often. The wedding and the reception were a nicely blended mix of the grooms' two very different backgrounds. Every table at the reception was a mixed crowd of both their respective families and friends. I enjoyed watching rich white people marvel at the crawfish étouffée in front of them. To be fair to the northerners who prepared the meal, it was pretty solid. Lord knows folks up north don't know a thing about Slap Ya Mama seasoning.

While I was ecstatic for Derrence and happy to reconnect with old classmates and friends, at no point did I stop that evening and think, "This could be me." This was Derrence and Nick's moment. I was just happy to see them happy, but not thinking that type of happiness was something I could have or even want.

However, the question would soon command larger scrutiny, as nearly a year after I attended that big, great gay wedding, on June 26, 2015, the Supreme Court made same-sex marriage legal nationwide. I've donated money to causes supporting marriage equality initiatives in various states and to nationwide efforts. I've written about marriage equality as part of my work as a political commentator. I've argued with various simpletons who struggle to understand that the religious fables they were told about marriage don't quite match up to the actual history of it. That Adam and Eve don't have a damn thing to do with marriage, and that "holy matrimony" began as a means to establish property rights. That marriage is determined by the state, not a church, and if the state can recognize common-law marriage without great protest, heterosexuals can shut themselves up and let the gays get married too. So, as far as justice goes, I was overjoyed when the Supreme Court ruled that every same-gender-loving individual had as much right to become a divorcée as the straights. Yet as a personal matter and for what the decision meant for my life, I wasn't moved. My friends surely were, though. I think a lot of that has to do with "love is love" so often being the uniting messaging behind equality for LGBTQ rights. I've long struggled with that, because there is more to me than who I love—and love itself is far more complicated than slogans make it out to be.

As soon as the ruling was announced, Kim, who, as you'll recall, is my closest friend from high school and one of the few folks from Houston I've managed to remain close to over the last twenty years, called me in complete jubilee. "Bitch, are you crying?" She very much was. Kim will tell you that she's a thug, and while there is indeed a Rap-A-Lot Records element to her, Chief Justice Roberts's choice not to be completely useless brought out the Céline Dion ballad in her. I loved how happy she was for me. I appreciated how much this historic moment meant to her as the friend of a gay man. Of course, I couldn't help but joke that I didn't have a man and so was in no position to get married anytime soon. Kim chuckled at the quip, but she remained optimistic about my future both individually and as a part of the community. More calls and texts came—including from those who recalled my self-described dream wedding from a drunken brunch. To their collective delight, I performed elation the way they wanted to hear it from me. It wasn't the time to piss on marriage and bring up my issues. Once again, I opted out of rocking the boat.

Before I even accepted that I was gay, I had already soured on the idea of ever getting married. It wasn't because I didn't think gay marriage was a possibility at the time. Even when marriage equality was nothing more than a pipe dream, I resented marriage and found it to be something that probably wouldn't work for me. I wish my hesitation had been majorly rooted in the question of whether or not such a heteronormative institution fit my gay ass or if expressing immediate glee over the Supreme Court ruling meant I was genuflecting to norms not designed with me in mind anyway. In panels, I've heard others shout about that while highlighting that polyamorous relationships and other kinds of romantic and sexual arrangements that break tradition should be exalted the same way monogamous relationships—like marriage—are. I feel their pain, but that ain't got shit to do with me. My uneasiness with marriage mirrors that of so many others: my parents' marriage haunts me.

My parents are still married, though I'm not particularly sure why. Granted, it's ultimately not my business, but as a by-product of their relationship, I reserve the right to remain both curious and puzzled. I usually say each is waiting for the other to die. Apparently, patience is a good way to prevent premeditated murder. Whenever I make this comment, people assume that I am being facetious. It's likely because I say it so matter-of-factly, but it's how I feel based on my observations and experiences. I constantly lived with the fear that my dad would make good on his threats to kill my mom. I'm surprised my mom hasn't killed *him*. I used to offer to be a character witness or an alibi if she needed one. I've made peace with the reality that as a victim of physical, verbal, and mental abuse, my dad is just a symptom of a disease that has soiled so many members of our family. I would not say I have forgiven him for the terror he put all of us through, but I have learned to accept the reasons why he ended up the way he did and love him in spite of that.

As a young adult, I asked my mother why she kept us in that household of madness. Why did she put up with him? Why didn't she free her own self from the burdens of being with him? I asked this when I was in college in order to deal with the resentment I had toward her for keeping us in that environment for so long. She responded that she simply didn't want to end up on welfare raising multiple kids. I couldn't argue with that. I was not trying to victim-blame. I just wanted clarity on what her thinking was. Likewise, I wanted to know if the pressures from work and marriage were why, though she may have loved her kids dearly, she wasn't always kind to us.

Though my dad often used to say, "Don't ever get married!" my mom never discouraged marriage. She encouraged it, albeit slanted toward holy matrimony with a woman. Bless her heart. She also encouraged my sister to get married. I don't recall my sister ever wanting to do so. She did, however. There was no formal wedding ceremony. She just casually told me she was married over the phone long after the fact—and right as she was on the verge of divorcing her husband. As she was telling me about the divorce, she mentioned that our mama was the one who had pushed for her to get married in the first place. My response was immediate. "Why would you listen to her?" My sister is amazing. She is one of the strongest, hardest-working people I have ever met. She is a remarkable human being. However, much like I saw with my folks, I looked at how remarkable people could be put through so much needless strain thanks to marriage. Well, with the wrong people, anyway.

The failure to learn how to love someone properly is a trait that has since been passed down to me. I know it isn't right to base the failures of your parents on anything you do, but we are all products of our living experiences. Generally, I didn't grow up seeing a lot of people in what I'd consider to be happy marriages. I barely saw married couples—period—outside of a few family members. When I think about the kind of commitment that most people associate with marriage, I think about people losing. Losing themselves, their dreams, or at the very least a part of their happiness. And though I really am happy gay people are making strides in our efforts to have our love recognized fairly in terms of property, taxes, and medical visits, I struggle to wrap my head around the idea of ever making that kind of move myself.

It took a while, but I finally started to say these things to people out loud, forgoing my fears of how jaded I sounded. But, as a believer in the mantra "You don't have to get ready if you stay ready," I would have my defensive talking points prepared. "If I don't end up with anyone or, like, get married and shit, I'll still lead a happy and fulfilling life." I may never be married, but that doesn't mean I've failed as a person. Nor does it mean being unmarried means I will be lonely.

A friend called me on something: "Why would you shut down the possibility before it even happens? That doesn't sound like you."

No, it doesn't. My preoccupation with making sure I never do to another what I think my father has done to my mother has made me needlessly cautious about entering an institution that I have found creates more problems than solves them. The fact that I have thought about this so much suggests that I'm already ahead of most people when it comes to taking marriage seriously.

Another challenge is that there are not litanies of healthy gay marriages out there to be held up and learned from. The bright side of this is that I might be able to set my own rules and boundaries— ones that work for me and my needs.

To that end, I can think of a few rules.

As previously acknowledged, he must accept Beyoncé as his lord and gyrator. I do not believe in Beytheism. No, no, no.

He must accept that I will probably always have a craving for fried catfish on Friday. Even if I do not eat fried catfish every Friday, he should not try to read me for craving it. That would be culturally insensitive.

He must not judge me for wanting to watch *Love & Hip Hop*

and *The Real Housewives*. The same goes for Lawrence O'Donnell's show on MSNBC. I feel like Lawrence is me as an old white guy and we have a spiritual bond mere mortals cannot fathom. And he better watch Joy-Ann Reid with me, although I've noticed she has developed quite a following with the gays because she serves more reads than a twenty-four-hour library.

He must understand my need to sing Kut Klose's "I Like" at least five times a week out loud. The same goes for Kelly Price's "Don't Say Goodbye." It's a thing for me.

Oh yes: #datass.

This doesn't mean I'm suddenly back to dreaming of a wedding day. I am still not addicted to the cult of marriage or preoccupied with the idea that it is a milestone that must be reached. I know so many straight people like this. Frankly, they all seem crazy as hell. But it is nice to know that for so long the rest of us have been deprived of this kind of crazy, and finally I get to partake in it too. And in doing so, I can shake off the stigmas I once applied to marriage because of the folks who made me. I don't have to let the past dictate my lifestyle choices. So if marriage happens, awesome; and if it doesn't, oh well . . .

Okay, one change of plans if it does happen: maybe instead of "Get Me Bodied," I should bop down the aisle to "Formation." That feels more appropriate.

The Pinkprint

I don't care about white people like that. That's not to say I carry with me some pointed, irrational hostility toward white people. Granted, when I find instances of white folks engaging in some sort of racist stunt, I will look at Black folks and other nonwhites, let out an audible sigh, and maybe voice a comment such as "White people!" But no, I do not specifically abhor white people. I spread my hatred evenly—the way God intended.

When I say I don't care about white people like that, I am referring to whiteness. Whiteness is why white people are placed at higher in the social hierarchy than everyone who isn't white. Whiteness fuels racism, and that racism is designed to protect whiteness and the aforementioned hierarchy at the expense of everyone else. Whiteness is so pervasive and so powerful that I have to explain that when I say, "I don't care about white people like that," I have to be very clear that I don't mean I hate all white people—because it would be catastrophic for me to utter such a declaration. White men and women can create media companies, businesses, and accrue political power based on anti-Blackness, but even though I would never want to do the same with some similar shtick centered around contempt for white people, the fact is that such an option would never be afforded to me in the first place, since only white people can hate without repercussions. Like that punk-ass forty-fifth president of the United States of America.

Whether white people want to admit it or not, whiteness by and large informs their outlook on everything. How could it not? They sit at the top of the food chain in society, so their standards are considered, well, the standard. Whiteness is so pervasive and so powerful that many make it seem as if whatever opinion whiteness and white people have is of greater value.

But I don't care about white people and whiteness like that, because I wasn't raised to pay white people and their whiteness much mind. This had to do with not being around white people much at all growing up. They were not prevalent in my neighborhood. Outside of middle school, I didn't see much of them in my K–12 schooling because I primarily attended predominantly Black and Latino schools growing up. Even when I was a magnet student and saw a handful of white students in middle school, we still didn't have the same classes.

I can remember three white teachers in my entire K–12 life: the first was a very young white woman who came across as one of those people who planned to teach at a Black school for a short spell before applying to law school (indeed, she was gone the following year); another taught choir and was very upset about O. J. Simpson's acquittal; the last one wasn't necessarily the Teena Marie of white teachers, but she definitely conveyed a level of comfort about being around a bunch of Black and brown faces. So, yeah, outside of those three and the handful of white kids in middle school, that was it.

Houston was an incredibly diverse city, but I saw white people only in doses depending on the setting. For example, I saw them at the Houston Livestock Show and Rodeo, because it was the sort of big event that brought people together. Then again, I only went to the rodeo on what was commonly referred to as "Black Night" because it featured performers like Luther Vandross, Gladys Knight, Destiny's Child (or Beyoncé once she went solo), Monica, and Brian McKnight, while also honoring the contributions of Black cowboys. So, yes, I saw a few white people the same way I saw them when I would go to the Galleria, the really nice mall with all the fancy department stores (as opposed to the "Black mall" known as Sharpstown a few mins away), or at AstroWorld, the now demolished amusement park, or maybe the museum or the zoo. But even in those instances, I recall few times when I ever interacted with white people. If I did, it was incredibly surface-level, because southerners are ultrapolite.

Much of this is rooted in socioeconomic status. As a Black person growing up working class, by default, white people didn't want to live by me, go to school with me, or be in most of the same social settings as me. My neighborhood and schools each represented the "inner city" that is so often discussed in media, but most frequently by white people who don't know the people in those spaces. We are treated dismissively: as products of our environment and as people whose fate is sealed. So, no, it's not about any bias, but merely seeing myself ignored and responding in kind.

I didn't fixate on white people and whiteness because it was well established that, as a collective, they found no value in me. Nevertheless, I knew Black people were of value. Despite not growing up wealthy and despite being effectively segregated by way of that status, my mother made it clear that Black people were not deficient. She took me to Black doctors and dentists as a child. Although she couldn't afford it, when she did want to place my brother and me in private school, it was the Imani School, a private Christian school run by the Windsor Village Methodist Church—a hugely popular and predominantly Black church. She was a devout Catholic, but she still wanted us to be at a Christian private school run by Black people. Yes, my mom told me about racism—not that it was a hard thing to figure out as an early news junkie—but while it was made clear that I may face certain obstacles, I could overcome them because I had already seen a wide variety of all the things Black folks could achieve on their own. In hindsight, my mom was preparing me for the times when I would be around white people—and whiteness made certain that I would enter those spaces with a sense of pride.

So this is what I mean by not caring about white people like that. Of course, I will always worry about interactions with law enforcement, as those pose life-threatening situations, but overall I look at white people like this: if you don't present prejudice and we can just enjoy each other, awesome; but if not, I will not let it eat me alive, because it's whiteness at work, and that's not my Black-ass problem. Yet as someone who now works in media, I realize that my situation is very different from that of many other people.

It requires a great degree of sacrifice to work in media. You are expected to intern for little money, if not for free, and then take an entry-level job that will not pay much and possibly lead you to question why you bothered getting a college degree. You do this under the impression that if you continue working hard, you will finally be compensated the way you deserve to be. Most people cannot afford such a sacrifice. Needless to say, I do not come from a background that lends itself to being able to afford such sacrifices, so in a lot of ways, I do find myself to be a bit of an anomaly among other Black media folks because even coming from a solidly middle-class or upper-middle-class background is a distinct advantage that I know nothing about. A lot of Black people in media come from worlds I only ever saw on TV when I was growing up. That is, they went to more diverse schools, if not predominantly white ones, whereas I went to Howard, *the* HBCU. They've had to deal with white people and whiteness for much longer, and while I would never make the sweeping generalization that all of them carry the burdens that come with being a Black person in a majorly white space, there are some who do. I feel for them, but I cannot relate to that. I'm lucky to even exist in this space with any of these people whose futures seemed more certain than mine.

I've learned over time that success in this world has a lot to do with one's proximity to whiteness. People overall value mainstream publications more than they do Black media. Part of that is rooted in folks knowing how difficult it is to be able to have your voice in mainstream outlets. Still, I want to be a success, and that entails placing myself in spaces different from those I'm accustomed to. The struggle with that, though, is that I am often asked to lead with my otherness. I don't walk into a space pronouncing to be Black or gay. I *happen* to be Black, and I *happen* to be gay. These things inform my perspective, but I don't believe either requires a great announcement. Still, when you are one of a few, you're typically asked to speak from those places.

Unfortunately, even when we are asked to write about our-selves, we are often asked to do so within even more rigid prisms. For instance, Black outlets and certain newer mainstream outlets run by younger editors will pretty much let me talk about whatever I want, however I want. (Well, minus the one time a Black male edi-tor younger than I was warned me about using turns of phrase that were too "in group." Translation: stop sounding so Black. He cared more about whiteness than I ever will, and I never wrote for him again. Problem solved.) In any event, with more traditional outlets, whenever commissioned to write about subject matter that's more personal, I've learned over time that the more pathos is involved, the better it will be received. You know, because it's so hard to be po' Black me.

Here are the topics mainstream outlets love for me to write about from the perspective of a gay Black man: Black homophobia; AIDS; and sexual racism. I don't mind confronting Black homophobia and transphobia, but it's always been twofold for me: I will condemn any mythology that suggests Black folks are magically more antigay or antitrans than white people, as if Black folks came over on a cruise ship clutching their Bibles while saying they couldn't wait to pick cotton and keep Luther Vandross in the closet while also calling out Black folks for trying to borrow white folks' oppressor baton and use it on issues related to sexuality and gender. As for the AIDS, well, yeah, I get it, and I try to confront the harsh realities of an epidemic that lingers on and on. With respect to sexual racism, I tend to cringe and roll my eyes so fervently that I'm always surprised that at least one of my eyeballs doesn't roll out of its socket to escape the abuse.

The reason why I roll my eyes is that I am supposed to take umbrage at the fact that I do not meet the sexual fantasies of a white man. Why? Because white men are the end-all, be-all, don't you know? How could I not be so offended to the point that I must address the matter over and over and over again. Then place the topic in my back pocket and pull it back out on command? #AllWhiteDicksMatter or whatever.

—

I remember the one and only time a white boy kissed me. Technically, it was two of them at the same time, but it was spawned by one of them because he kept calling me "beautiful" in an accent that I couldn't quite place. I can make out a British accent, a German accent, a French accent, and maybe an Australian accent, but outside of that, I'm clueless. The best I can do is say the dude sounded like one of the men Jason Bourne beat the shit out of in *The Bourne Supremacy*. Anyway, it didn't matter where his speech pattern stemmed from, given that he mainly communicated with me with his tongue. It happened at some white gay club in New York that I never would have gone to if I weren't with Samuel, someone I met through a scholarship program who was visiting the city at the same time I was back for another internship. Samuel was Mexican and from Los Angeles, but he was clearly no stranger to the Blacks and was very good at clocking a homosexual. I thought Samuel was a snack when I first greeted him, but I wasn't out, so I never said anything. By the time we did link up, I learned he had quite the appetite for white men, which is why we hung out: he wanted to go to clubs my gay friends from the same area as me in Houston were not at all interested in going to.

Samuel, who called me "girl" every thirty seconds, was high out of his mind, and wanted me to at least get drunk so we could go to some spot in Chelsea. The spot was massive and full of shirtless, no-body-having white boys and quite loudly played that kind of music that just thumps and requires a glow stick and Ecstasy to appreciate. I didn't want either, so I had lots of vodka to deal with it. By drink number infinity and beyond, I found my way to the dance floor, and not long after, into that triple kiss. The one who called me beautiful was the one who kissed me first, then had me kiss his friend, and then had me kiss the both of them at the same time. Then he kept kissing me. He also grabbed my dick a lot.

I hung out with Sam a couple of days later, and once again, it was at some gay bar populated mainly by white gays. I realized Sam's affinity for white men was partially influenced by the access that it provided. He liked white men with money, and regardless of what many gay white men dealt with in terms of homophobia, they remained white men and commanded a kind of social capital that only white men could. Being on the arm of white privilege had its perks, and he enjoyed them. I still did not like those clubs. The lil' triple kiss was fun, but I wasn't toned enough to leap around shirtless, and if I was at a dance club, I wanted to hear music I could dance to. You cannot body roll to techno, or at least body roll in the manner that I'm accustomed to. Not to mention, Sam got most of the attention and was bound to ditch me.

I wasn't sure initially if not being paid much mind in the white gay clubs was directly related to racism. A lot of people have told me that I look unapproachable. I appreciate this one straight Black man who was comfortable enough with his sexuality to tell me, "Yo, bro. You do have resting bitch voice. Cut that shit out, bro." I do the best I can, but I normally have to end up approaching people as a result of my being seen as unapproachable. Having said that, I do know the type of men I attract, and they are overwhelmingly not white. Anecdotally, the running logic between my friends and me is that in terms of aesthetic, American white men want Black coffee, no sugar, no milk, while the European ones are more into café au lait.

I never honestly thought about all this at great length until I had been asked by multiple editors on several occasions if I had some story to tell. And then if I had any others. I know that within the last couple of years, there has been a personal essay boom. There is also an insatiable need for content and a desperate need for clicks. All of this explains why across various outlets—but for sure gay publications that are mostly run by white men—there is a constant overflow of pieces penned by Black men lamenting white men who don't find them sexually attractive.

Most of them read the same:

Oh, white bae, why don't you love me?

Please, baby, baby, baby, please, white zaddy, want me. The way I want you.

Give me that pumpkin-spice-latte-loving penis; I need it.

The same goes for white men who write pieces claiming that their stance against dating Black men—"It's just my preference"—does not make them racist by default. For the record, yes the fuck it does.

Of course, because video matters more to media outlets with each passing quarter of lackluster advertising revenue, these diatribes have now been flipped to videos. As if the essays weren't painful enough reads . . . Either way, they're heavy-handed and hard for me to read.

Look, I understand the frustration. Sexual racism is wrong, and I get that this is a long-standing issue. I know that people should make sure bigots know they cannot cower behind the false pretense of preference. Yet I am sick of reading and watching Black men complain about white men not wanting them sexually. I loathe the immediate assumption that I care that much about whether or not white men find me sexually attractive. You would think that Martin Luther King had a dream that one day a Black dick and a pink dick would sword fight and then finish all over the rainbow flag.

All too often, when it comes to tackling the relationships between gay Black men and gay white men, it is discussed widely within the context of sexual attraction. This places whiteness on a high pedestal and plays into the pathology of minorities. *Aww, this Black boy just wants some of that pink print. Poor him.* I realize that the topic will never disappear because racism is stubborn in that way, but I do find the emphasis on this conversation to be stifling. There are plenty of ways to discuss disparities between white men who don't identify as straight and their nonwhite counterparts outside of whether or not the latter meets the standards of the former.

For instance, in 2015, the *Advocate* published an essay entitled "Is Gay Dating Racism Creating a Black HIV Crisis?" To his credit, the author of the piece, Daniel Reynolds, did ultimately speak to someone from the CDC who explained that other factors played a larger role, but the problem with the piece (and there have been many more pieces since then published along that narrative line) was that it did not frame the topic within the right context. Indeed, two years before that was published, the *New York Times* published a report, "Poor Black and Hispanic Men Are the Face of H.I.V.," which examined factors behind higher HIV rates among poorer Black and Latino men. In it, they detailed how Black and Latino gay men were less likely to take drugs before having sex and were no more likely to engage in risky behavior than their white gay counterparts but that our infection rates were higher all the same. The reason behind the problem at hand had nothing to do with sexual racism and everything to do with the failure of health organizations to reach both groups.

Months after reading that essay in the *Advocate*, I got an email from the National Alliance of State and Territorial AIDS Directors (NASTAD) announcing the launch of a new online training platform to "help doctors, nurses, and medical professionals unlearn racial bias and elevate the quality of health care for Black gay men and Black men who have sex with men." In the press release for this initiative, Omoro Omoighe, associate director of health equity and health care access at NASTAD, said, "There is a lot of discussion right now about implicit bias and police brutality in the US—but the truth is, this is a huge challenge for health care providers as well."

For the first few years I lived in Harlem, I walked up and down 125th Street nearly every day. There are a lot of reasons to hate walking up and down 125th. Despite New Yorkers' reputation for being fast walkers, it's a damn lie, along the same lines as "Winters here ain't that bad." There are also the constant cries of "BLACK MAN, LET ME HOLD A DOLLAR!" Sometimes I do give them a dollar if I have one on me, or I'll at least buy someone standing homeless outside of that Dunkin' Donuts on Lenox coffee and/or a breakfast sandwich, but when I don't have it, damn, you ain't gotta cuss at me! I can't forget the men from the Nation of Islam trying to hand me the latest edition of the *Final Call* that blasts white folks while the religion itself maintains homophobic views. It literally takes everything in me not to hear one of them call me "brother" without yelling, "Y'ALL DON'T LIKE ME EITHER, NIGGA!" Sometimes I just want to rap along and bop to Nicki Minaj in peace, you know?

What has grated on my nerves the most about 125th Street is that I have only once been asked if I wanted to take an HIV test. Harlem and Washington Heights have some of the highest HIV rates in the area. Where are the people regularly handing out condoms and encouraging tests? Why should I only be offered either during Harlem Pride? I can get a fish sandwich from a solar-powered truck on 125th. I can go to Whole Foods and get some organic chicken wings, turkey legs, and surprisingly well-made macaroni and cheese. Random folks will ask me if I have a kid who needs a checkup or teeth cleaning. If I can get all of that, why can't I get some genuine health outreach?

So when the CDC now claims one in two gay Black men will acquire HIV in their lifetimes, whatever is in someone's Grindr box is inconsequential to a problem that is a crisis and can directly impact my life. We can talk about sexual racism, but do not center the fate of a minority health crisis on the sexual desires of white men. To wit, when I finally did start to see ads for PrEP in the Harlem area, they predominantly featured white gay men or white gay men with Black gay men. They couldn't have at least one Black couple together? In Harlem, of all places!

Interracial relationships are perfectly fine. I could never fault them, because they gave us Mariah Carey and Barack Obama. In the same way Will Smith and Omar Lopez helped me figure out that I liked boys more than girls, the same goes for Joey Lawrence, his brother Matthew Lawrence, and Jonathan Taylor Thomas. There are some white men whom I find attractive. I would still take Ryan Phillippe down, and Nick Jonas is more than welcome to join us. Having said that, the imagery isn't lost on me. It does ultimately cause people to believe that is the standard, or at least a type of relationship worth aspiring to have. A white man not wanting me is not be-all and end-all, though. At this point, I find this topic boring, and I never want to be asked about it again. Why be so focused on the "preferences" of racists? Why help feed the ego of whiteness by centering it? I'd rather run my head into a wall several times with Ronald Reagan's racist "welfare queen" speech loudly playing in the background than boo-hoo about not being Black enough for a white boy to want me.

If someone's "preference" is that I am not good enough, oh well. It's their loss. It doesn't require that much of my energy. Someone who values you less will not be convinced by your public crying about wanting to belong. I am less interested in wanting to belong and more passionate about being equal. Not being treated equally is why HIV is a greater reality in my lifetime than it is in the life of a white man. We have to stop giving other people's preferences so much power. We need to value ourselves so much that no outside force, no prejudice—even one disguised as preference—can make us feel second place.

I suppose I learned this early, because as a little Black boy growing up without wealth in the South, whiteness and white people were already far removed from me. I already knew what price they placed on me, and it was very little. But I didn't need them to tell me of my worth. I want others to have this same feeling, because if you are a nonwhite person measuring any part of your value based on a system predicated on diminishing you and all those like you, you are on a fool's errand. You can't win by their metric. It's not designed with you in mind.

I treat every man—Black, white, Latino, Asian, Middle Eastern, indigenous, or whatever the lovely melting pot of bae miscegenation created—who doesn't want me the same way: fuck him, I'm cute.

I'll Dial That Number

The nightmare has always been the same. My father has reached the maximum potency of his alcohol-induced rage fest, and the main target for his wrath is his wife and my mother. Words are exchanged between the two of them, his profanity-laced tirades shifting to threats on her life, and then it happens: he tries to make good on his threats. I'm present in the room as he attacks her, as he tries to fulfill his long-standing promise to murder her, but I am paralyzed. For the life of me, I can't get to her. I can't stop him from trying to kill her. I am immobile, stuck watching the unthinkable happen right before me and helpless to stop it. Seconds before she looks to be leaving this world, I am quickly awakened. The reaction to the dream is always the same too: I'm always shaken by what has just happened, and for a few moments, I lie there in my devastation, in my feelings of failure over not being able to stop the tragedy.

These nightmares started when I was child and have followed me through my teenage years and my twenties. As for my thirties, they've happened only three times: on back-to-back nights during a trip home for Christmas, and another time when I was visiting a friend who had just suffered the loss of his mother.

As much as I love my family, my hometown of Houston, and the friends I still have there, it can be hard for me to go home. Time and distance have helped, but it is difficult to revisit not only the scene of the crimes but also the visible damage the events that happened in our home have had on the house itself.

There was always a buildup to his acting out. My dad, who never exhibited an appreciation for standing still, usually hung around outside, where he could move around with the freedom that his penchant for constant mobility commanded. When he was out there, he'd be cutting the grass—maybe for the billionth time that week—or tending to the flower beds. Or he'd be working on his old truck. Or he'd be standing outside blasting music—anything from Johnnie Taylor to the Isley Brothers to Barry White to whatever CD he'd pulled out of my sister's car to help him stay current. There was a period when he played Master P's *Ghetto D* album constantly.

He was never alone, though. He was always surrounded by people: friends and "friends" alike. They were playing dominoes, some of them smoking, and of course there was a lot of shit-talking happening. Some of those acquaintances presented as friends, but as time went on, all it might take was one miscommunication for an argument to occur—one that may or may not have led to blows. Much of that could be attributed to alcohol, of which there was no short supply. Vodka. Cognac. Beer. His "water," as he'd call so many things. If it wasn't someone else that triggered his anger, it was the baggage he carried inside of him. My father was a land mine, and the last thing a person like that needed was to self-medicate with alcohol. But when you didn't have the tools to deal with all that had happened to you, you turned to whatever vice you needed in order to get through the seconds, minutes, and hours of a given day. You turned to it when you thought about moments of the previous days, months, years, and decades that continued to torment you. And then you repeated the cycle of your abusers by taking out what ailed you on those closest to you.

My mom served that role; therefore, he would direct his venom at her. Trivial shit would be the jumping point: what she cooked and how it was not like his cooking, what she didn't cook for him because he suddenly forgot how to cook his own meals, or that she didn't want to engage his almost childlike need for attention and validation. Not feeding into whatever he felt he needed led to the slamming of cabinets and doors, and then to the snippy remarks. These were all the actions of someone fishing for a reason to be mad and lash out.

My dad could be an intimidating presence, but I never witnessed my mom display fear of him. If anything, she mostly responded to his antics by ignoring them. As he screamed, she responded with silence. We all mirrored her response. It was better to pay him no mind rather than allow him the chance to spoil everyone else's mood. But he was so vigilant in his attempts to get a rise out of her, to get her to say something back, to give himself a reason to make it more than it ever needed to be. That was why, after a certain point, he would often manage to get under her skin and get her to respond to his cruelty in kind. My mom was adept at knowing just what to say to fuck his head up, so when he ushered her to her breaking point, she would send him into an even greater tizzy. Once that happened, he would really get going.

"Fuck you, Di."

"I'mma kill you, Di."

"Die, bitch."

"I swear in the name of the Father, Son, Holy Ghost I'm going to kill you."

"Dial nine-one-one. I'll shoot at them too."

"Fuck all y'all."

These were classic lines from the usual script. He would subject us to blasphemous rants intended to make light of my mom's devout Catholic faith. This only made him appear all the more like the devil. He also often used to shout about resenting not just marriage but having a family too. I long suspected that neither of them had envisioned being married to each other, much less with a family that effectively kept them bundled together out of financial necessity, but if there had been any lingering doubt, he made sure to confirm it. I didn't doubt that he loved us, but that didn't excuse his behavior. The darkness inside of him and his commitment to cruelty were displayed even more when he would point out the abuse that my mother had endured as a teenager. How did a man do that to his wife and the mother of his children? How did any person do that to even a *stranger*?

And then there were the times he struck her. We would often huddle around her in the living room in preparation for the moment he might dare to do so, because if he jumped on her, we would all jump on him. That was why he would holler about 911, daring us to dial that number. I vividly remember the one time one of us actually did. He snatched the phone and broke it. The police came anyway. Before answering the door, he hid the guns he had in our home. Once he made his way outside, he put on a show. He was actively resisting arrest. I peeked out through the blinds from the bedroom that my brother and I shared. He was in handcuffs, leaning on the car trying to kick his feet in the air to fight off being put inside the police car. He ultimately was placed in the back seat and spent the night in jail.

The very next day, I had to get up and go to school. While waiting at the bus stop, a kid named Joe mentioned that he had heard what had happened. I'm sure everyone had. My dad was a very loud person who made sure he knew every single person surrounding us. Yes, that might make him a good neighbor, but that also meant what I had long suspected: most people knew how he was and could hear his tirades in the middle of the night almost as well as we could. It was embarrassing, and something I never talked about. On that morning, as Joe mentioned him to me, it was clear that even if I wasn't talking about myself, others might be.

My dad never let us forget the fact that 911 had been called on him. He used it as fodder for future fits and fights. He resented us for what he felt was our having turned on him. That took a lot of nerve, given that he was both parent and tyrant. He never owned what he did; he only gave excuses.

Shortly after many of these arguments, he'd enter our rooms to talk about his past. He had been abused as a child. His father would beat him profusely—even holding up a loaded shotgun to his chest. They lived in a house out in the woods in a tiny town called Raywood, Texas. There were not a lot of people around. The homes were not even in close proximity to one another. Still, you could apparently hear my dad's screams from the beatings given by his father. Those were calls for help—help he never got.

"He fucked with me," my dad once explained on his knees, full of tears, and red beyond belief.

Sometimes he managed to get me to cry along with him. The sympathy would soon dissipate, because he would go back to bothering my mom and keeping us all up for the rest of the night until he decided to go to bed. It was selfish and vile, and those tears were emotionally manipulative. Yes, he provided context for why he was the way he was, but at some point, you had to make a choice to do better. After all, wasn't he cognizant of the underlying issues?

But again, he didn't know any better. A lot of the beatings he had endured had occurred because he was trying to defend his mother. I don't know exactly what happened because no one really speaks on any of this, but I've heard his mother ran off and left him there with his father, his abuser. I used to see his mom growing up, but that stopped after a while. It's a shame not having a connection with members of a such a large family, but it's a mess of other people's making that I have no interest in righting. I don't even remember what my dad's father looks like. There are no pictures of him in my home. I know his name was Nelson, and my sister told me that he used to love me. I have no recollection of that, and I don't care. He was a monster that brought havoc, and that trait was passed on like the shape of one's nose.

The frequency of these outbursts varied. Sometimes it would be every few weeks, but in other instances, every couple of months. They always happened during the holidays, though—notably Mother's Day, Father's Day, and especially Thanksgiving and Christmas. I love Thanksgiving and Christmas, but for as much eagerness as I had for those holidays, there was also trepidation over whether or not he would let his demons ruin our celebrations, as they had ruined so many other things.

We used to have other kids over. That was, until this one time when my father argued with my mother in the kitchen, grabbed her by the shoulders, and viciously pushed her back and forth against the kitchen cabinets. I was around ten. I didn't let anyone come over my house after that, minus one time a decade later—and even then I couldn't enjoy myself because I was on pins and needles about my dad's behavior.

Other fears followed me into adulthood. I didn't drink until I was twenty-one. Of course, that was the legal age, but I worried so much about becoming an alcoholic like my dad. I knew I was susceptible to addiction because of the number of blood relatives I had who were addicts. I'm thankful for my high tolerance, yet I have to make sure I don't drink when in any sort of volatile state, because that paves the way to addiction.

My dad's rants about marriage stuck with me. I struggled with getting close to people. I worried that I could potentially bring that kind of pain to someone else, so I was always wary of getting close to someone—even when I was in pursuit of men. It wasn't until my thirties that I had an epiphany: I was attracting unattainable people because I was no less unattainable. I didn't want to be alone, but I didn't know how to let my guard all the way down. I knew how to volunteer the kind of information that gave folks the sense of connection; it was a tactic to throw them off the scent of who I really was and what ate away at me. I became even better at it, because the few times I felt I was trying to get close to people, they rejected me or used what I had divulged against me. That deepened my underlying cynicism that falling in love with someone opened the door for them to destroy parts—or all—of me.

That was how I saw my parents. I imagined that whatever love they had for each other wasn't enough to overcome their own respective issues. I knew I was not my parents, but I also knew how easy it would be to become like them. In life, people will disappoint you, but the key is to learn how to find within yourself a sense of peace and confidence that keeps you whole during the times when you are let down.

I wanted to be better than my father. I didn't want to repeat the cycle. I became obsessed with not doing so, but not necessarily with doing the work to unlearn things, to settle my feelings, and, most of all, to let go of my anger.

I spent much of my childhood wishing my dad were dead. I understood that I was considered fortunate to have a two-parent household; people would tell me as much. However, because they did not live in that house and endure what we did because of my dad's unsettled trauma and alcoholism, they couldn't get how incredibly stupid that sentiment was when expressed to me. I did not feel lucky. I hated him. I hated him so much that I wanted to kill him. I wanted to kill him so much that I carved "DIE DAD AND MOM" into the wall of my childhood bedroom. Him because he was a menace, and her because sometimes I would blame her for keeping us there or because she wasn't always kind herself. Still, most of that fury was aimed at him. I knew how I wanted to kill him to boot. My dad always kept a knife near him. He kept one underneath his bed. I used to fantasize about taking that knife from under his bed and stabbing him profusely until he took his last breath. I thought about that as a *child*. *That* is how much I resented him. Once, while he was cursing at my mom and threatening her and then the rest of us, I looked him in the eye and told him what I wanted to do. I couldn't do it, of course, but even the fact that I thought about it still troubles me deeply.

Whenever I go home and sleep in my old room, I sleep beside

that carving made in the wall. I loathe seeing it. I tried to scratch it out once, but it's carved in so deep that it can't be totally erased. Neither can the memory of my doing it. I hated him so much because none of us deserved that, especially not my mom.

I had to get away for college, both for my big dreams and for a much-needed escape. Of course, my problems followed me. I was a combination of my parents in that I could keep cool like my mom— up to a certain point—but I could also blow up just as ferociously as my father. I kidded myself into thinking I could control that residual anger. Suppression was not the answer; forgiveness was. Even so, despite knowing that I needed to change, there remained the rightful presumption that my dad was incapable of giving me a proper sense of calm or closure.

He was never going to admit wrongdoing. He was not going to say, "I'm an alcoholic and I'm going to get help." I had already heard those false declarations as a kid. He was not the kind of person who opened up in that way. Nor would he ever say, "I'm sorry for the pain I caused your mom, your sister, and your brother."

My dad was also never going to take ownership of having stalled my acting career. As a kid, I used to be in plays in both elementary and middle school. Of course, the one time that my mom appeared to be fed up with my dad enough to divorce him was when I was in middle school and interested in such things. Seemingly unable to stomach his ass any longer, she took us all to our grandparents' house in the middle of the night. After that, we stayed at our aunt's house. Based on the way she was talking to us, she truly seemed fed up. Then my dad followed us: first to our aunt's, and then he rolled up on me at my middle school. I spoke to him but scurried the hell away, because I figured I could be done with him for good. That proved not to be the case. We ended up back at home, and barely any time passed before he huffed and puffed and blew all that same bullshit back at us.

This was near the end of my eighth-grade year, and I was applying to schools. My grades were slipping and my conduct was the worst because I was lashing out at teachers—cursing at them in some cases—and getting into fights. My only real shot at avoiding my zoned school was HSPVA, the performing-arts school in Houston. Naturally, my dad acted a fool damn near to the very day I had to go and audition. I ended up blowing my audition and didn't get in. In my mind, had I gotten in, I would have perfected my craft and gone on to have a successful acting career. I mean, that could have been me playing Bobby Brown in BET's New Edition biopic (I would have tanned). If not, I could have settled on Ronnie DeVoe. But no, my dad took that away—and it was another thing he wasn't going to apologize for.

We're not a family sitcom about an affable, affluent family trying to solve life's greatest hurdles in twenty-two minutes, so I had to minimize my expectations. My dad was an old-ass Black man who was not afraid to hurt people, and like many people—including myself—he had been raised not to talk about his problems but instead to pretend that they didn't exist. The idea was to keep going in spite of them, without admitting that no amount of running from your problems or feigning amnesia about them would prevent them from catching up to you one way or another.

I had to create my own level of closure. First, I had to see my dad in totality. He wasn't all bad growing up. I liked the trips he took my brother and me on, where we could catch fish and crabs. I remember the smiles on our faces when he would filet the fish after we were done and fry everything in the back of his truck. Cooking had always been his way to show affection: the gumbo, the barbecuing, the chicken strips that I obsessed over and always asked for. The fast food he would buy me even though he kept complaining about how expensive it was and that we had food at the house. I appreciated when he would buy the basketball rims, the baseball stuff, and the punching bag. I understood that he tried to be present in the ways that he could be. These gestures did not absolve him or cancel out my fears that one day he might get too drunk and angry and do the unconscionable. But reflecting on the whole story helped, because I was able to humanize him and not only view him at his worst.

I didn't forget anything that had happened, but making the conscious choice not to cling to the past as much as I used to do was helpful. As was giving the man the benefit of the doubt. Moreover, if I wanted to have a better rapport with him, I had to make some effort myself. Every so often he would call me, not to talk at length but just to see if I was alive and if I needed anything. He always said the same thing: "I'll dial that number if you need something, boy." At those times, I barely recognized who the hell was on the other end of that line, and it was a genuine gesture that I often promptly shooed away. He routinely said, "I'll give you my last." He would preface it sometimes with "I'm just a poor man, but . . ." or something similar, but no matter how he said it, he did mean it.

The intent was to show that he wanted to be there for me in some way, because I was physically present only once or twice a year. When I was, he would turn back to cooking. So I would eat those smoked turkey legs he made for me. When he asked if I needed food, I stopped snipping "No" and went with, "Well, can you gon' 'head and get some seafood boudin and put it on the pit?"

One time, my dad also offered to stab anyone who might have been fucking with me. Honestly, that was sweet for an old, thuggish man who truly would try to fight you even in his sixties. Around this same time, he also called me his nigga. I wish they made greeting cards for statements like that.

I've learned to call him on my own without prodding from my mom. I've learned to call him and wish him a happy Father's Day and sound sincere about it. And I now call every so often simply to say hello. The calls do not last long. He'll ask how I'm doing, mention the weather, and once again ask if I need to "dial that number." Most times he's pleasant, though there are instances when he bemoans that my siblings and I favor our mom over him. "Y'all's ya mama's boys" is what he'll say. I don't fall for the bait, and the second I think I'm going to regress and get irritated, I change the subject or end the call. We don't necessarily know how to hold extensive conversations, but being able to have the short ones we do is significant progress. That's mostly attributed to my ending the call with "Love you, Pop." We were never really in the habit of saying "I love you." I always maintained the position that I loved him for giving me life, but left it at that. Now I don't say "I love you" with any asterisk. I love him, as complicated a figure as he is. And he now says it without my pushing him to do so. It's not that I ever doubted he loved me, but I gather it's not something he was used to saying out loud.

He continues to drink, but as far as his rage goes, age has slowed him down. I don't know if he's tired of the fighting or just tired. It's long been time for him to stop, all the same.

I've come to learn that a lot of things he can't say to me out loud are said to my sister, whom he calls most. Years ago, I did a video for a media outlet about my coming-out story. A first cousin from his side of the family found me online through my writing. First, she tried LinkedIn, which I often forget exists, and then she found me on Facebook, where she watched the video. In it, I was blunt about my experiences and my parents' reactions. So my cousin went to my dad and said, "Your sons are gay and it's your fault because you're an alcoholic." My dad did not call me about this. Frankly, I think he knew better than to come to me with it. Instead, he called my sister and said, "I know my boys are gay. It's not my fault, though, and I don't care as long as they're happy."

"He said that?!" I asked her.

My sister said that he had indeed. He also relayed a familiar claim: "I'm not an alcoholic. Alcoholics can't take care of their families." He thinks being functional in one's addiction negates said addiction. I don't bother with that now. Watch your mouth and your hands with my mama and do whatever you want with your liquor.

That's another thing I've learned to do: indulge him when he offers me alcohol. I understand how dicey that is. I worry about whether I'm enabling him. But I've settled on accepting that there are things about him that I cannot change. And I'm not going to turn down free booze. I'm also more inclined to accept his offering because he did not shun me when confronted by some cousin whom I've seen twice in nearly twenty years' time.

My sister informed me of something else too. I never talked with her about our uncle until I was barely thirty-three. I told her that I remember vividly how our father reacted to Daniel's death and all of the "faggot"s he hurled after the funeral. She didn't remember that. I told her that she probably wouldn't because it wouldn't have affected her in the same way. Having said that, some days later, she said she vaguely remembered some of it, only she filled me in on more details about their relationship. She explained to me that my dad and Daniel were incredibly close, to the point where Daniel lived with my parents for a minute. It was her theory that my dad's reaction, as I recalled it, had more to do with his own hurt than anger directed at me. That made sense, given his pattern.

There are still some questions that linger in my head. I wonder if he, like me, had those same nightmares of his father killing his mother. Was he also so angry that he wanted to do the worst to his dad in retaliation? Has it ever hit him that he's repeated some of his dad's own mistakes, and if so, did he worry about his own children having a similar fate? I'd ask these questions if I thought I'd get answers. I wouldn't, so I won't.

I do know a few things. I know that in spite of his faults, he is a funny, charismatic, hardworking man. When my friends would pick me up to go out in high school, most of them would note how cool my dad, who introduced himself as "Doc," was to them. An eye roll was the response I'd give them, given that they had no idea what was going on, but in the interest of fairness, I will admit now that his ass always has been cool. You see it in his old pictures.

I also know that he is proud of me. He's never read anything I've written, bless his heart, but he doesn't know how to use a computer and rues the day he got a smartphone. But I know that he knows I have worked hard to create a life for myself, and as a man, he respects that. He admires what I've accomplished, and I know this based on how his friends know that I went to Howard, that I lived in LA and New York, and that I've gone a lot farther than most people who grew up around us. The one and only time he's been on a plane was to see me graduate from college. He needed a tranquilizer in order to sit still for the flight. Washington, DC, was an unrecognizable world to him, but thanks to the hotel workers, whom he managed to befriend fast and who told him that he looked like Katt Williams, he enjoyed a certain familiarity and comfort.

Most of all, I know he knows that when I used to look at him eye to eye, love was not in my sight. But now when I say "I love you" over the phone or before hugging him good-bye as I leave Houston again, he knows I mean it.

When I look in the mirror, I mostly see my mom's face, but from certain angles and with certain expressions, my dad is there too. In the past, this would make me angry or bring me to near tears because when I saw that in myself, I saw a nightmare. I have worked hard to successfully shake that off. If I hadn't reckoned with my past, it surely would have continued hindering me in the present and future. As I've learned with my dad, no one is completely good or bad, and many of us carry the potential for monstrosity. Whether or not we give in to this is determined by how we deal with our demons. My sense is that my dad was born with an ebullient spirit that was literally beaten out of him. My long-standing fear was that it would be taken away from me based on how I was raised. But that too was just something I finally needed to let go.

The Impossible

hris, the same friend who, a few years prior, had told me that
my dick was dry and suggested I turn to technology in order
to have a more active sex life, apparently believed that my penis was
better moisturized now, which led him to offer me new advice.

"I really just want you to settle down with a nice Black man," my
personal Iyanla Vanzant explained. "It's time, Michael."

I immediately thought of old episodes of *Living Single*, in which
Regine Hunter's mom would constantly call on her to "settle down
and put some buns in that oven." Chris's comment was both an encouragement to seek a relationship and a thinly veiled reference to a
noticeable shift in the sort of men I had been dating. Before moving
to New York, sans for that one Asian dude who I had thought was
mixed but turned out to have merely braided his hair and gotten a
grill and chosen a name that screamed Negro League, I dated Black
American men exclusively. It wasn't that I didn't find other types
of men attractive. Again, anyone attractive can get it. However, in
terms of the sort of men I had been around socially and who re-

sponded to my advances, they primarily had been men who looked like me and whose experiences mirrored my own.

Something changed when I got to New York City. It's not as if I suddenly became repellant to Black men or repulsed by them. Throughout all these quips from my friends, I had dated a few. Still, it was Latino men who started to be the most responsive; who wanted follow-up dates; who engaged me as much as I sought to engage them; who wanted to have sex. Some of this was due to the fact that I lived uptown, where there were a lot of Puerto Ricans and Dominicans. When I first got here in 2005 to intern, people kept walking up to me and speaking Spanish. Outside of being able to tell them my name and most of the days of the week, I was lost. My old pre-AP Spanish teacher would probably be so disappointed in me. Once I moved here, the Spanish-speaking only seemed to occur more frequently, so I did learn how to say one thing in particular: *"No soy dominicano."*

As for dating Black American men in the city, my experiences have been a little muddied. Sexually, I've attracted them, but in terms of dating and trying to forge something more substantive, it's been different and more difficult for me. One scrolled through my social media accounts as we were talking, caught a glimpse of me on television talking about Beyoncé, and concluded that I was too "feminine"—well, he said he didn't do "feminine tops." I do not call myself a top. I do not call myself a bottom. I have a preference and can be selfish if I don't care that much about you, but I don't lead with that preference in the context of dating, because I'm in my thirties and asking someone whether they're top, bottom, or verse seems tacky and simple. That's just a fake-ass progressive way of me saying if we're not in a relationship and you don't nag me to bottom because of love, it's not going to happen, because that shit is painful and only Ja Rule believes "pain is love." So, yeah, unless we're in a deeply committed relationship that includes obnoxious IG vacation photos, good luck booking that night of me bottoming you speak of.

There is also the issue of dating men who don't have a college degrees, which sometimes results in slick comments about my being "oh-so-smart." Or there are the educated men—often with more degrees than me—who know I am educated but do not find me as, uh, *cultured* as they are.

I sometimes felt that way at Howard. Although I ended up loving the school in the end, when I first got there, I met people from "Houston" who were more from the suburbs. They'd hear where I was from and what high school I had gone to and would react snootily. Once, a girl said, "Ohmigod, you're from Hiram Clarke and you went to Madison and you're at Howard with me? I'm so proud of you!" It was a patronizing pat on the head. *You little hood booger, look at you managing to be around the likes of me.*

I can't forget the one guy that I really, really liked. We hung out a little bit, and then all of a sudden he said he wasn't focused on dating. Naturally, he had a boyfriend from Houston a few months later, and he gleefully told me this via text. A year and change went by, and all of a sudden we started to run into each other again. I told him it was Beyoncé telling him to take the hint. We started hanging out once more. A few months later, he ended up telling me during the birthday dinner I treated him to that while he found me attractive and thought of me as a "great catch," he thought we would be better as friends. "You're like a lawyer, in that even if you don't believe what you're saying, you will say it with conviction for the sake of being right. Like, you need to be right. And I'm emotional, so that wouldn't go well."

I raised my hand as if I were in class and asked him if I had ever done anything to give him the impression that I would operate that way in a relationship. "No, but I just have a feeling." *Man, fuck your feeling.* I did go ahead and treat him to the dinner, but I wanted the universe to reach down and trip him from the stool he was sitting on as he projected his own insecurities onto me.

I do not always need to be right. I don't like to argue. I won't necessarily back down from a given stance, but I do not have a problem being wrong. Being told you're wrong means you're being given an opportunity to better yourself and be more knowledgeable. I try not to speak without an informed opinion, but if that opinion can be shifted, if not flat-out discounted, for the sake of enlightenment . . . proceed, motherfucker, proceed. It's fine.

In other cases, weird circumstances got in the way of dating. As in, *We click, but you're moving to Los Angeles next month, so this is a waste of both our time.* Or there is a vibe, but then you find out your friend blew me two years ago, and while that should not matter, it does to you, so fine, cancel the wedding I'm already planning in my head.

—

I'd always been wary of talking about this out loud, but I did make an attempt to address these issues in a piece about single life for a major newspaper's online vertical. I wanted to write a nuanced piece about dating outside your immediate pool. I wanted to make clear that I was not a social studies failure, so I was fully aware of the differences between nationality, race, and ethnicity. Being Black and growing up in this country often requires you to explain yourself in ways that you shouldn't have to. I wanted to make sure my piece didn't mirror any of the essays that I'd read from Black people complaining about other Black people who didn't want to date them, essays that fell into familiar tropes like "I was told I wasn't Black enough because I grew up listening to the Smashing Pumpkins" or some bullshit like that. Same goes for people who were obviously dealing with self-loathing. I didn't want people thinking that I hated myself, or that I hated Black features, or that I found certain ethnic groups to be superior. I didn't want to be lumped in with folks who thought that way. Those types tended to have Black Republican hairstyles: for Black men, a cut that lacked a proper lineup, or for Black women, some dry-looking ball of hair tied together in a way that screamed, "Help me find a hairdresser, my Democratic sister."

My intent in the piece was to convey that I used to feel it was important for gay Black men to be seen to be romantically involved with other gay Black men. However, as someone who wrote so much about gay Black male representation in mass media and what was lacking in it, I might have been seen as a hypocrite, because my own life didn't reflect this line of thinking. When I told a heterosexual friend of mine who was dating a white man about this, she told me, "I feel like that daily. I'm in my first healthy relationship, and it's with a white guy."

My goal was to write something that essentially said I had to learn to stop thinkpiecing my life and to stop clinging to ideals that didn't matter so long as I was happy. That was all I wanted. And I thought I had accomplished this until the editing process started. With all due respect, I do not ever need a white woman to tell me, a Black man, that I might sound "a little stereotypical, like a caricature of a person" because I mentioned a crawfish boil, Hennessy, boudin, and Abita beer. I am from Houston, Texas. My last name is

Arceneaux. My entire family was either born in Louisiana or was the first or second generation out of it. And Houston ain't that far from Louisiana anyway.

Worse, the headline that the publication chose made it seem as if I never dated Black men. After I complained about this, it was changed to imply that I didn't date Black men most of the time. I never told my editor any of these things. I am always very clear with my words and intentions. She saw what she wanted to see anyway. She tried to make me into the very stereotype I was trying to avoid. I already knew that close-minded white editors needed to learn how to let nonwhite people control their own narratives and stop pathologizing us, so the only lesson I took away from that experience was that I didn't need to explain myself to begin with. Now, when my friends crack their lil' jokes, I tell them, "I respond to the market," and extend them the invitation to shut the fuck up and mind their business.

—

The market led me to Adrián twice. The first time was via Grindr, a forum in which I never anticipate meeting anyone who will end up being of any significance to me. I downloaded the app because I was bored, horny, and needed a distraction. It was the summer of 2015, and after moving to New York and doing well for myself work-wise, I faced a common problem but under dire circumstances. A Black media outlet that I was contributing to both in print and online stopped paying me. Because my relationships with many of the staff members had turned personal, my usual "bitch better have my money" stance subsided a little bit and I gave the accounting office, stationed outside of New York, more time. That was a mistake.

They ended up owing me several thousand dollars by then, and I was devastated. I used Grindr to pass the time and get a release, but that was also around the same time said app produced the guy who brought fleas and/or bedbugs to my goddamn apartment. I wasn't really using the app to have sex anymore. Just to pass the moments between sending increasingly aggressive emails about my state of pay while trying to get work elsewhere.

Still, Adrián and I chatted for a bit. We exchanged numbers. We texted awhile. I could tell he was smart because he, like me, wrote in complete sentences. Some folks don't care for formalities in such settings. I respect everyone's lifestyle choices, but I prefer to write in a way that would make my old English teachers smile.

We were supposed to hang out but never did. I wasn't in the mood to be around people back then. Adrián did hit me up out of the blue one time to let me know he was right by my place if I wanted to hang or chill out. I brushed him off. I told him I was going to see Nicki Minaj in concert—a purchase I had made for myself and dré before this Black media outlet decided to enrage my Black ass by owing me all that money. I could have followed up with Adrián, but I didn't. I felt too much like a loser in those moments and was paranoid that the next time I invited someone over, they might bring rabies with them.

The following January, I recognized his face on Twitter after he tweeted me. I was better off by then and had a clearer mind, so after recognizing him, I slid in his DMs like a thirsty thot who knew he had made a mistake. I had a new phone, but I still had his number. He reminded me that I had ignored him for Nicki Minaj. He let me know exactly what I had missed out on. I was hoping for a second chance, so I asked him out.

We met at some Italian restaurant on the Lower East Side that was full of white people but that blasted a whole lot of Future. When we were texting each other, it was flirtatious, and I got the sense that we were going to hit it off.

We did not hit it off. When I arrived, he was waiting at the bar, wearing a black sweater and black-framed glasses that perfectly fit his face. He was beautiful but cold. He went from flirty and suggestive texts—and even a tweet about what kind of underwear he was wearing—to greeting me like I was the archnemesis on *Real Housewives* that Production forced him to sit with to film a scene that everyone knew would end in explosive confrontation.

It wasn't explosive, but it turned contentious when politics came up. We were right at the point of the Democratic presidential primary at which people were starting to vote.

Picture it: me drinking brown liquor and hoping to come across as charming when the conversation shifts to politics. I explain that while I am not especially fond of Hillary Clinton, I do feel that after the New Hampshire primary, she was most likely to win the states and delegates necessary to become the Democratic nominee for president. I add that Clinton is more likely to accomplish her agenda given that, months ago, she unveiled a plan to capitalize on Obama's use of executive power. I said that unless President Bernie Sanders tramples Capitol Hill like Godzilla, killing everyone in office so that we can start over in some politician-less paradise, chances were slimmer than a Bad Boy royalty check that homeboy would get much done as an executive.

You'd have thought I said, "Fuck Bernie Sanders, fuck you, and fuck you hippy-dippy assholes standing in the way of reasonable pragmatism with your strain of idealism that should be rolled into a

big-ass blunt." Sure, when the Sanders insurgency campaign started
to ramp up, I had found myself liking him enough to make a campaign donation that could have otherwise gone toward the purchase
of a catfish dinner with two sides and peach cobbler for dessert. Did
I think he was going to win the nomination? Hardy har. *No*. But
Adrián did, and considering he was a politically informed social
worker who loathed most American politicians (as someone from
Puerto Rico, one can see why he would loathe the government of a
colonial power), it made sense that he was one of Bernie Sanders's
most ardent supporters. We had a heated back-and-forth about it,
and despite his attempts to get me to Feel the Bern more, all I could
feel was myself going flaccid. It didn't help that he started talking
about how much he hated people touching him.

In my mind, I was like, *But you said . . . and you showed me
that . . . and you . . .* He smiled a lot during all of this. I'd never
seen a more beautiful smile on a man (my nieces win for best smile
ever, FYI). But beyond that smile, he was trolling the fuck out of me.
Enter Beyoncé, whom he trashed to get a rise out of me. I told him
that I didn't partake in Beytheism, so I would not engage in this
and I'd pray for his taste levels, but he kept pressing, and eventually
I went back and forth with him about that, too.

We took the same train back uptown. It was crowded. We didn't
even get to sit down. We just stood near each other. He reminded me
how much he hated to be touched. So, I barely touched him when
I got off at my stop and let him go to the Bronx. Of all the strange
dates I'd had, this ranked high. But I somehow remained curious
about him.

dré was puzzled by my lingering interest. "Wait, you still want
to see him?" I said yes, and so Adrián and I ended up grabbing

drinks again. And then again. And then again. And we texted a lot. We communicated a lot on Twitter too. He wanted to read my writing—which was new—and he continued to troll me as a Hillary bot while I encouraged him to enjoy the ride until Hillary slapped Bernie back to the Senate. After a while, he did let me know a few things. One, he was purposely fucking with me on date one: "I'm a lot, so I need people to prepare for that." He also casually let me know that he was HIV-positive.

For a subject that had scared me for so much of my life, by the time he made that disclosure, it didn't alarm me. Before I met Adrián, I was interested in someone else who I knew was positive. Someone "regular Black," if that matters (it does not). I thought that thing was going somewhere until he suddenly flipped the script on me. He was now celibate and wanted to know if we could just be friends. I didn't know why people bothered saying that. There are some people who can meet others under nonplatonic circumstances and go on to forge a lovely platonic relationship. I am not one of those people. I have friends. I don't want to have sex with my friends; therefore, you're *not* my friend. It's bullshit.

To wit, days after that guy gave me that speech, I saw him on Tinder. Just say you don't want me and leave it at that.

It's sort of funny how all of your life you have this great fear of something, only when you confront it, overcome it, and shake off those stigmas, you end up being told, "Eh, I don't want you." Life is funny that way. But that dude turned out to be someone whom I liked the idea of, versus who he actually was. This was not the case with Adrián. I found him to be gorgeous, smart, hilarious, and challenging in the best way imaginable. He constantly told me things that I needed to do or even write about. He was usually right. I hadn't known him that long, but I did feel that he was the sort of man that I needed to be around. He made me want to be better. He once invited me to Popeyes! Do you know how special it is to have a beautiful, intelligent, funny man hit your text like, "Wanna meet at Popeyes?" Bitch! That is how my ideal romantic comedy begins.

Unfortunately, we were both dating other people at the time, and as I would soon learn, it was more serious on his end than on mine. He invited me to a restaurant called Angel of Harlem, where he was having after-work drinks with his friend. After a while, he randomly inserted that he now had a boyfriend, but that we could be still be friends. I downed my drink, asked for the bill, paid, and turned to leave.

"Don't be a brat," Adrián said.

My response was that I wasn't being a brat, I was being an adult.

I had already been here before. I was not about to allow yet another person to know that I was interested but also allow them not to commit to me. I felt like I had already wasted so much time trying to make something of a situation that was clearly not meant to be. Additionally, I had already messed around in the past with someone who had a boyfriend. Living life like an SWV song was not the way to be. No, I needed to find something that was mine. Adrián had made a choice and it was not me, so I wanted to get away from him before I ended up getting hurt.

When I left, I thought that would be the last time I saw him. He didn't stop hitting me up, though. I didn't stop responding either. Soon, I was back to hitting him up. It proved all too easy for me to break that pledge to myself. He came to my birthday party, and I took him out to a Puerto Rican restaurant for his birthday fifteen days later. Still, I made it clear that this was going to have to end. The plan was for him to take me to some Puerto Rican restaurant in East Harlem that he loved for what was essentially a farewell dinner. But that dinner never happened. It kept getting pushed back. Instead, we met weekly for drinks. We texted nearly every single day. He sometimes called me out of the blue. He warned me that even if I blocked him on every social media platform and on my phone, somehow, he was going to show up to something I was doing and roll up on me like, "What's up?" I never tested him on that because I kept engaging him. While all of this was going on, I was actively trying to date other people. None of them were like him, and even when I tried not to compare anyone else to him, anything that lacked that same spark led me to do so.

He was different from me, but we had more in common than I initially assumed we would. What I came to learn dating men of Dominican or Puerto Rican descent (or, in his case, someone born in Puerto Rico) was how much they reminded me of country Black people in the South. I have joked that most Dominicans and Puerto Ricans are just Black people who order pig's feet in Spanish, but through Adrián, who did acknowledge his African lineage, I got a better understanding of why older Black women always gravitate toward Latin men. I was tickled that he had learned English in the 2000s from, like, Céline Dion, and didn't watch Black Americans on screen until TV shows such as *The Parkers* and films like *Two Can Play That Game* made their way to PR. He obsessed over both of those things. However, he clapped his hands when he was mad like every hood Black girl I'd ever met. He grew up playing dominoes with his dad the same way I had played with mine. I learned that when he said, "Pero, like . . . ," he was doing his equivalent of every Black girl and gay who loves to begin statements with "BUT I MEAN . . ." in an elevated voice.

He loved his dad the way I loved my mom. Once, he compared me to his dad while we were at a bar, which somehow led to us both tearing up in front of cat daddies in the middle of a Saturday. What I liked most about him and what kept me so close despite my misgivings was that for the first time, I felt as if I was being seen without having to tell so much. With Adrián, there was a level of comfort and ease that I'd never experienced with anyone else. I didn't have to say much, which was fine because, by and large, he had such a big, magnetic personality that I relished consuming him and all that energy. I learned all this in the months we spent together—which turned into a year, then longer.

We did differ in some ways. I tried to control my anger while he was a bit of a hothead, ready to go at a moment's notice. He thought Britney Spears's *In the Zone* album was her finest work and trashed me for liking *Blackout* so much. He only pretended to loathe Beyoncé, whereas I thought anyone who even pretended to entertain Beytheism needed psychiatric treatment. We'd each endured our fair share of trauma, but despite our both having a fair share of cynicism, I tried to fight mine off, whereas he mainly gave in.

He told me the story of how he had contracted HIV: his live-in boyfriend cheated on him with his best friend. A best friend he shared a tattoo with, sleeping with a man I assume Adrián thought he was going to be with for the long haul. I knew the betrayal bothered him, but I didn't know the extent to which it did.

As for why he didn't eventually choose me, he gave a number of different reasons. The first was to note that he was dating someone else and it was someone he felt was going to be his boyfriend. To me, he shouldn't have bothered dating anyone if that was the case, but such was his right. In any event, as he pointedly said back when he first told me about this boyfriend, "When I wanted you, you rejected me." When he told me that he had a boyfriend, I did wonder if the way he behaved on our first date wasn't so much about testing if I could handle him as much as it was having me feel bad about making a mistake. He admittedly liked attention. That didn't seem right. Neither was the other excuse: "I have to be the star in the relationship, and I wouldn't be that with you." Or that I was "annoying." Adrián annoyed the everlasting shit out of me too, but we both cared about each other, and we each enjoyed each other's company. That wasn't it either.

It wasn't until we decided to spend a little of the Fourth of July together that we ran into a few of our friends. Again, Black women love this DeBarge-looking Rican, so my friend Sade and her Virginia Black mannerisms meshed swimmingly with his PR-produced theatrics. Sade had already heard about Adrián. All of my close friends had. They remembered seeing him at my birthday party. People who worried about my feelings were not in love with this predicament that I had placed myself in, but they were more or less letting me cook in a mess of my own making.

As I got up to talk to some other friends I saw, Adrián and Sade had their own conversation. I wasn't sure how he decided to pour out to her about us despite not knowing her well, but she circled back to me about something he had hinted at but had never completely explained. He often joked about having the "kitty" and dying, but I didn't feel he truly believed that. However, it was clear to me after talking to Sade that the manner in which he had contracted HIV may have permanently altered his outlook on love and relationships.

He would go on to tell me that "You would want a real relationship, and I cannot give you that." I got a better understanding of why he hadn't picked me. His boyfriend, whom he curiously started referring to as his "roommate" not long after this, gave him what he described as "security." I didn't know what they had. I didn't want to know what they had. It is likely for the best that I never know. He made such a big case about what he assumed I would or would not deal with, but the fact was, he never gave me a chance to prove myself. Rejection hurt anyway, but with him, it was all the more painful because I'd never felt so connected to someone, and I wanted him so badly. Painful because I knew it had to end. Painful because regardless of whether or not he declared otherwise, I did have a say as to whether or not he could stick around. He'd admitted that he'd been selfish to an extent, but I had been a willing participant. I wouldn't be one forever.

I wish it had been different. I don't like regrets, but I do wonder if I hadn't ignored him the first time things might have been different. That it might have been me with him. I might have had the opportunity to show him that I could be whatever he needed, so long as he continued being what he'd been to me. But every choice I'd made was right at the time. And maybe we were only meant to share those moments in order to guide us to the next stages of our lives.

If time and space will allow it, maybe there will be another chance. If that isn't meant to be, I'll carry with me the good feelings he gave me and the faith he restored in me as a result of it. I'm not sure when I'll settle down with a nice man. It still depends on the market. And, above all, honest communication.

I Can't Date Jesus

"**Y**ou care too much about what I think," she said matter-of-factly as I tried to get my emotions back under control.

Adrián had gone to the bathroom, and the mezcal I had kept ordering had given me the liquid courage to call my mom and get something off my chest. I had told myself that I wasn't going to bother with her anymore. That she believed what she believed about homosexuality, and no amount of engagement would alter that.

After coming out to my mom at twenty-five and being met with a disapproving, callous response, I didn't discuss my sexuality with her any further. That was, until I felt the need to warn her that there would be a personal essay from me appearing in *Essence* magazine based on something gay-related—one that would include my picture as well as my byline. It was my way of saying, *Our last name is not common, and I look exactly like you; therefore, prepare yourself for the likelihood that while you're getting your hair done, someone is going to pick up a copy of the magazine—with Oprah, of all people, on the cover—read through it, and possibly turn to you and say, "Is this your (gay) son?"* It also doubled as my way of making clear that based on this cover and a few other placements of my work around that time, I was actively working on boosting my profile—meaning more folks would know more about my work and the identity that informed it. I was fairly blunt, and, from time to time, that bluntness could be read as vulgarity. For my friends in Houston, that outspokenness could sometimes be a bit much, so they offered a suggestion: before I said something that they might think of as outlandish, I had to say, "Brace yourselves."

On this call, I was trying to let my mom know that if all went to plan, more folks would know about me, and that would include knowing about my sexuality. So, yeah, ma'am, get good and ready.

I tried to be civil with my approach. I tried to talk about God and difference of opinion. I stressed that I thought that no matter how she felt, especially about how I had stopped going to church, I felt that God was using me in some way to help create dialogue. To try to bring people like us together. To not simply regurgitate dogma but to explore it, challenge it, and not be so selective in what we believed. Biblical literalists of convenience had long bothered me. My irritation only heightened upon learning more about the six scriptures in the Bible: how they were idioms of their time; how the analogies and metaphors had largely been misinterpreted; how other Biblical texts had been used to subjugate Black people and women. I was hoping she would see the parallels now with her gay son. She didn't want to hear any of that. She was a person who missed the pre–Vatican II era in which tradition reigned supreme, down to masses being performed in Latin. She did not want discourse; she wanted me to quit resisting. After I had laid out my thoughts on the

call, she offered a response that mirrored the one she had given me
three years before.

"Am I happy that you're gay? No. I'm sorry it happened to you.
Am I hurt that you're still gay? Yes, because I feel responsible."

She then went on to lament about the state of the world, how
"people" were trying to "use" folks to make what was "not okay seem
okay," but stressed that in "the eyes of God, it's still wrong." I had to
put my phone on mute for a second so I could get out every "shit,"
"damn," and "motherfucker" before I could continue this conversation. Did she honestly believe that I was a sucker allowing myself to
be made into a prop? Had she met me? She, of all people, should
have known that everything I said or did was of my own volition.
She oughta have known this because I wouldn't have been a Howard
grad, an ex–LA transient, or a current Harlemite had I listened to
her. I could not have done any of those things without her support,
but no matter how strongly my mom spoke out against a choice I was
making, if it was something I had decided was best for me, no one,
including her, would steer me away from what I felt was the right call.

And there was some bit about "the family" potentially abandoning me. She meant her side of the family, the only extended family I
could say I knew well enough. I loved all of them, but I couldn't have
given any less of a fuck if any of them resented me over my being gay.
What were they going to do? Tell me that I couldn't have any of the
cornbread dressing at Christmas because dressing was only for people who didn't commit adultery? I asked my mom what position any
of them would be in to judge me anyway. She had no retort, though
it didn't matter anyway, because none of them have said anything
to me about my being gay. If anything, they were concerned about

my well-being and rooted for me. It wasn't about them. No, this was her issue. She was more concerned about how a boastful gay son reflected on her.

As the conversation went on, she went there: she said she knew that I had been born gay and that I couldn't help who I was. She was a nurse. She liked science. She was smart. She got that people were who they were. But she was a devout Catholic. Religion could make you suspend your better sensibilities. Its success in making the faithful fall in line no matter how foolhardy a position appeared was rooted in how great a role faith played in people's lives.

I admired my mother for a number of reasons, but what I admired most about her was her strength. She was the strongest human being I had ever met. She did not need to be loud to be commanding. She did not have to be aggressive to convey how tough she was. I knew that strength stemmed from her faith. Her religion kept her going. It was her guiding light as she steered through all the murkiness her life had faced. I appreciated her dedication to her faith. I respected it. Sadly, she refused to see that her religion stifled me. I couldn't follow Catholicism the way she did. Her version of Jesus suggested that though He may have loved me, He merely tolerated me. The mantra "Hate the sin, love the sinner" troubled me, because if you were under the impression that being gay was inherently wrong, you were operating from the frame of mind that *I* was inherently wrong. You thought I was the human equivalent of irregular denim bought at an outlet mall. I was nobody's clearance-ass jean; my packaging was fine.

She didn't think that way because she fell in line with the church's teachings. It was why despite admitting for the first time to me that she knew I couldn't help who I was, she advocated for suppression. She cautioned me to not act on my urges. She remained afraid of what could happen to me after I died if I dared to live.

"You could act on them, go outside, and get hit by a bus—and I won't know where you're going."

She didn't want me to go to hell but couldn't see that to not be wholly human might fit my own version of hell on earth. Why would I acquiesce to the Catholic Church anyway? They were still trying to clean up the mess they had made by knowingly shuffling all those boy fondlers around for decades instead of rightly expelling them. A mess that could have been cleaned up much sooner if they had abandoned that silly vow of chastity they forced on priests and that even sillier clinging to patriarchy that prevented them from recruiting from the big pool of women who majorly populated their churches. The only insight I could get from the Vatican at this point included shoe recommendations and where to buy one of those bad-bitch dresses priests were required to wear while performing mass if I ever decided to switch up my style.

Knowing all this, I told her that I hadn't a doubt in my mind that if a bus hit me in the next few minutes and I died, hell was not my next and final stop. She wasn't convinced. She stayed on that "please, baby-baby, please accede to church doctrine" stance.

I so desperately wanted to scream back, *Well, girl, I can't date Jesus.*

My mom always talked about heaven. She loved the idea that no matter how much suffering we endured in this world, we would be rewarded in the afterlife if we just lived up to certain ideals. Once, I stopped her in the middle of one of those paeans to say, "It sounds like you're waiting to die to live. You can have a bit of heaven now before life here ends." She smiled but didn't really offer a real response.

We were alike in many ways, but therein lay the difference between us: I didn't want to wait until I was dead to get what I felt my soul was due. I preferred to go for it now rather than live life by rules I found restrictive and that, based on one gigantic maybe, may yield a reward once I was dead.

The call ended with my mom telling me that she loved me and wouldn't abandon me. Even so, her discomfort was palpable. She couldn't understand why I felt compelled to "tell everybody my business." That registered as code for "I don't get why you have to tell the world you're gay and embarrass me."

After that conversation, we once again found ourselves not speaking. My mom usually called me every year on my birthday a little after 3:27 p.m. Central Standard Time—the time of my birth. As she said year after year, it was not my birthday until that moment. I looked forward to those calls so much. But that exchange we had was a few weeks before my birthday. My thirtieth birthday rolled around, and she did not call me. Hours went by and not a word from my mom. Even my dad called! I ended up calling her. She didn't hide her disapproval and lingering irritation with me, enraging me and nearly ruining what thankfully turned out to be a birthday full of love. My friends made up for it, and I ended up enjoying the night in spite of the hurt.

That hurt didn't go away, though. I felt it the next morning. And the one after that. And the one after that. It took time to shake that off. True enough, she never technically abandoned me. In her own way, she was always pushing me to keep going. She didn't want me to flounder. But even if someone loves you, it's not the same thing as loving all that you are.

I know my mom loves me, but I'm just as aware that she always had a different vision for my life. Ideally, I'd be working in a more secure field (finance, corporate law, medicine), one that would make all her sacrifices worth it. I would also be straight and married with kids. We'd all attend mass regularly, and she'd have us over for Sunday dinners. I might even be back in Houston. Maybe not directly under her, but close enough (in Houston, traveling long distances within the city limits is normal). But I am none of these things. I will never be any of these things.

Not being those things makes me worry about how much I may be disappointing her. I fear that I have because I've chosen a much more difficult path. One that requires a lot of sacrifices for a reward that may or may not come; and if it does, it will come a lot later than expected. To add "being gay" to the list and knowing that as a gay Black man certain health risks remain only heightens that worry.

—

During the summer of 2011, I was going through one of the most difficult periods of my life. I was abruptly let go from a site I was writing for in a permalance capacity (that means they want nearly or exactly full-time work but are too cheap to give you benefits, so you have to buy your own), and though I found freelance roles elsewhere, most of the outlets were not paying in a timely manner, and I was owed thousands of dollars. Such was the life of a contractor at times. Beyond those headaches, I noticed that I was experiencing actual headaches that made it difficult to stand up without wanting to fall back down in a ball of pain. On top of that, I was breaking out into rashes. They started on my hands and arms and then quickly spread to other parts of my body. The rashes on my arms did not look like the ones on my legs. The rashes on my legs did not resemble the rashes on my back. My lips started to have black spots too.

Thankfully, I had insurance by this time. A couple of months prior to this, an ear infection had led me to a county hospital in Torrance, California, as I had been recently been kicked off my mom's plan. The first time I went to the ER, I was told the wait would be so long that it would probably make more sense for me to come very early the next morning to make certain that I would get treated. So I did, and I was, but while speaking to my mom about insurance in the parking lot, I noticed a bunch of juveniles circling my car. Those badass kids didn't think I knew what was happening. I almost ran all of their asses over. My mom said it was time for me to get a gun; I reminded her that California's gun laws were stricter than the ones in Texas, so in the interim, I just needed to go ahead and call Blue Shield back.

Pre-Obamacare insurance for a single gay man in his twenties was pretty great at the time, so I went to see a dermatologist fast. Bless my heart, I didn't ask Black people for a recommendation first. That gave way to some polite white woman who looked like Diane Keaton's second cousin but treated me as if she got her medical degree from the Damn Fool School of Medicine.

"Oh, my God! You look just like Chris Rock. I bet you get that all the time!"

Actually, no, I don't. Back during All-Star Weekend there was a little boy at the bus stop outside of my apartment complex running behind me yelling, "Chris Brown! Chris Brown!" A few bus drivers and waiters made the same mistake back in 2009. That's the only Chris I've been compared to in the past, and to be honest, I don't see that one either, outside of us both being lanky and brothers in big teeth. After settling her underlying question—DO ALL BLACK PEOPLE LOOK ALIKE?—she said something about sun allergies and then offered another opinion: my rashes might be related to syphilis.

"Don't you have to have sex to get an STD?"

I wasn't a virgin, but I was not fucking a soul. She said she was just "throwing it out there," but that I should get it checked all the same. She also suggested that I might suffer from a common inflammatory disease and that I should have a biopsy done. I came back for that, and before they scraped my skin to get tested, she turned to the nurse and said, "Doesn't he look like Chris Rock?" Madam, why are you back on this nonsense? The Latina nurse shook her head no. I did not have whatever skin disease she talked about. I also did not have syphilis. I told her that's a good thing, as it would be unfair to have the effects of relentless weed smoking without the benefits of any high, and the same goes for having symptoms of a sexually transmitted disease without any of the fun first. She laughed. I was serious. Maybe she knew that. At least all that was settled. Unfortunately, the migraines were still there, and fatigue coupled with body aches tagged themselves in for a pile-on. After giving me a cream for the rashes, she recommended that I go see a doctor downstairs about the rest.

That doctor was an old white man who looked elderly enough to long for the days he could say "colored" instead of "African American." Additionally, he appeared surprised that I—this young Black boy—was in his office. As he asked me to describe my symptoms, he suddenly made an interjection.

"Are you a homosexual?"

I told him yes, and then he proceeded to tell me that I should have some blood work done in order to check out if I had hepatitis C. I didn't know where that had come from, but it spooked the shit out of me. He said it so cavalierly too. As if that was what happened to people like me.

I had been keeping my mom abreast of everything that was

happening, but when I heard "hepatitis C," I panicked. That doctor's office was in the Larchmont area of Los Angeles. As soon as I walked out of that building, I sat on the sidewalk directly in front to call my mom. My mom was one of the few people I felt comfortable being emotional with. I wasted no time in starting to cry. My mom may have introduced me to Black doctors and dentists as a child, but over time, I'd had other doctors of different backgrounds. However, she only took me to doctors whom she knew and who knew her as a nurse. So, as I was describing the way he spoke to me and the shift in tone and demeanor after he asked if I was gay, she tried to be comforting but nonetheless noted that the reality was, with that admission came the chance that you would be subjected to people's prejudices—prejudices that multiplied when you were dually Other.

As for the hepatitis C, I was mortified. All that suppression of urges. All that denying myself pleasure out of fear of contracting something that could end my life prematurely. All the damn blue balls I had given folks initiating something sexual only to pull my dick away as a result of my outstanding paranoia. Imagine not giving in to your feelings out of a protectionist mind-set only to find yourself in a feared scenario anyway.

My mom tried to be encouraging.

"I don't think you have hepatitis C, but even if you do, while it's not curable, you can have a full life. We can figure it out. And look at Pamela Anderson. She has it. She's okay."

My response was me choking on my crying and barely audibly quipping, "BUT SHE LOOKS TERRIBLE." That was more down to styling and makeup than anything, but it made sense to me in that moment (Pamela Anderson has since said she's been cured, so my bad, sis). For more than a week, I worried about what my life would be like if that doctor's warning rang true. I called constantly trying to get answers.

When I finally got called back in, it was a Black dude who handled the blood who told me that I didn't have hepatitis C. He looked puzzled when I asked him about it. As if that should have never been on my mind. That same doctor from before came into the room and then gave me that similar look. I reminded him that it was something he'd led with.

"It was only a possibility. I didn't think that was likely."

Bitch, why in the fuck didn't you say that at the time, ho?!

He said that while my liver levels were off, there was nothing that gave him great concern. He then suggested that much of my problems could be related to anxiety and stress, so he prescribed Xanax. I took one of those at night and couldn't open my mouth fully without being in pain for a month and change. I was experiencing teeth grinding during all of this, but Xanax only exacerbated the problem. For the record, only Celexa and Klonopin treat me right.

I will hate that motherfucker forever. A few weeks after all of this, I saw his old ass working out at the gym. I wanted to trip him on the treadmill, but the universe stopped me. I hated him for seemingly reacting to what he saw as a gay mannerism by throwing out the possibility that I had something incurable that would lessen the chances of me living past my fifties. I hated him because that fear made me turn to my mom and worry her. My mom had had to endure far more pain than any person should ever have experienced, especially a person as beautiful, generous, and loving as she was. I felt like I was piling on.

I didn't want to disappoint her. I didn't want her to feel guilty and make her feel as if keeping us in the home with our father was responsible for behavior that she didn't approve of.

I don't know why she stayed with my dad. It's not for me to know. However, I know part of it is the family she made with him and needing to take care of us as best she could. She's sacrificed a lot of her life for us; the least I can do is make her proud. To succeed. To be healthy. To not give her more reason to worry about me in a world that already provides ample reasons for a mother to worry about her Black children. In the end, all of this guilt I've carried with me is centered on not wanting to fail my mother.

I can escape fault over a misdiagnosis and someone else's biases. I am guiltless in that sense. But to choose writing for a living and to be unabashedly gay and write about being unabashedly gay and learning to reject the interpretations of Christian doctrines she lives by: that's all on me. I have to be who I am, but how does one reconcile that with who she is?

What happens when I fall in love and enter not a situationship but something that is purely mine? Will she not want to meet him? Will she shun me again? How will I react if she does?

When Hurricane Harvey hit, I frantically stalked my family to make sure everyone was safe. On the night when the rain consumed the entire city of Houston, a little after midnight, I called both my mom and sister. You could hear the terror in their voices. They did have reason to worry. My aunt had to be rescued by Coast Guard helicopter. Other relatives had to be rescued. I noticed days later, a friend from high school had lost her brother and sister-in-law in the flooding. My sister had a two-story home, so she was safer than my mom. She wanted my parents to come to her house, but my mom didn't want to go.

Still, she was scared. "I've been through many hurricanes and storms before, but nothing like this, Michael."

There was a specific way she pronounced my name. Her Lafayette, Louisiana, accent had remained pure in spite of decades of distance. I didn't allow myself to think this would be the last time I would hear her say my name, but in the days after, when I knew everyone was safe, I reminded myself of the fragility of life. My mom could be a bit morbid. She was always talking about death. Part of that was waiting for heaven. Her reward for doing what she felt was right and living by what she felt was God's will. I hated thinking about my mom not being here anymore. But the older she got, the harder it was to push such inevitability aside.

I want my mom to be here forever, but if that's too much to ask, I want her to stick around for as long as possible. I only wish that we could reach some sort of accord about that part of my life. I want her to embrace that part of me and engage with me about it. I want that wound to close. I have to accept that it may never close. But while I don't want to feel like I am failing her, I have to acknowledge that she's right: I care too much about what she thinks. She may be my hero, but we have very different ideas about how we get to heaven. I hope she reaches hers, and I hope I have mine. If she never changes the way she feels, it's her mistake—one I can't keep trying to fix.

If nothing else, I want her to know that I wouldn't be who I am if not for her. My dreams would have died long ago if not for her support. And I hope she knows that I know that no matter what has been said, it came from a place of love and concern. Neither one of us has ever wanted to let the other down. That's always been a testament to how much we love each other.

Sweet Potato Saddam

"It's hard to wake up to a reality that so many people hate you." It was days after the 2016 presidential election, and this white gay man couldn't believe that bigotry was so rampant in the United States of America. The fact that an apricot-hued asshole ran a vile campaign engulfed in racism, sexism, xenophobia, and audacious idiocy and was handed the presidency was unfathomable to him. I smiled when he said this and proceeded to raise my Black hand and rub my skin.

Trust me, I know the feeling.

This was exactly why, as much as I wanted to see my new gay white friend and allow tequila the chance to temporarily pull me out from under post-election stresses at his happy-hour mixer, I was wary about going. When it came to my closer friends—you know, "the Blacks," as he referred to us—many of them didn't want to talk about it at all after a while. After the initial shock, most of them needed a pause. Not many were ready to deal with what the election results signified.

What frustrated me then and what has frustrated me every single day since is that we're supposed to believe that what happened was that anomalous. Yes, a self-righteous FBI director made an impact. As did a hostile foreign power adept at catfishing on a budget by way of social media. The same goes for a superficial, profit-driven media more invested in the spectacle of a bigoted reality star huckster managing to get this far.

However, as surprising as the result was, in the end, all Russia did was exploit the racial biases America has never truly addressed. Voter suppression had just as much to do with Hillary Clinton's defeat as James Comey did, if not more. Overall, fragile white people in desperate need of an ego boost are why he won. It's a reminder that after eight years of a scandal-free Black president and his gorgeous, dignified family, white folks voted for a malignant-narcissistic sociopath with no political experience as his successor. A man whose political legitimacy was only achieved after he jumped on and further publicized a conspiracy theory that questioned President Obama's legitimacy as an American citizen. A man with the intellectual curiosity of a dead gnat whose purported fortune was secured not by his self-professed business acumen but by the licensing of his name, which only managed to mean anything again thanks to an NBC game show. A serial liar and an admitted sexual assaulter. References in various rap songs from Black folks who just wanted to denote wealth and went with the known blabbermouth with lingering mythology notwithstanding, we never liked that asshole. We've long known he was racist. We knew what "law and order" meant. We never forgot what he said about the Central Park Five. A lot of us were aware of his sordid history with housing discrimination. Birtherism was still fresh on all of our minds.

He won all the same. He sold a white electorate the dream of returning the country to the state in which Black people, Latinos, and Muslims all knew their places, where immigration was out of sight and out of mind, in which queer and trans people were relegated to dark corners and closets rather than standing tall on television or using the bathrooms of their choice. And, overall, he made white people feel less fragile about their standing in America (no matter how deluded such questions about it were). The revisionist history about the campaign that promptly began after the election results would be hysterical if not for the dangers it imposed on the rest of us.

All the election did was give anyone who can be deemed "other" a reminder that we are all hated that much. Yet we were collectively encouraged to give the president-elect a chance. I admire the graciousness of "Crooked Hillary's" concession speech. She declared that man "is going to be our president" and that "we owe him an open mind and the chance to lead." I liked the purple suit she wore that morning, but not enough to believe that bullshit. I don't even like saying that jackass's name. Since he won, I've intentionally tried to avoid using his name, and whenever an editor has allowed me the chance to not use it, I've put something else in its place.

A list of every name I have used instead of the one on his birth certificate:

Tangerine Mussolini

Habanero Hitler

Minute Maid Mao

Honeysuckle Lenin

Sunkist Stalin

Sweet Potato Saddam

Bankruptcy Batista

Carrot Cake Chávez

Real Estate Hitler

Sweet Potato Pie Satan

Orange Moon

Peachy Pol Pot

Sunny D Zedong

Tropicana Jong-il

Colby-Jack Führer

Mandarin Orange Mugabe

Papaya Batista

Parmesan Putin

Hoghead Cheese Hussein

Garlic Bread Gorbachev

Because fuck him. I owe him as much respect as he gave anyone not white, male, straight, and rich during the campaign: none. The same goes for his supporters. So many people in media—all of them white—have asked us to give his supporters the benefit of the doubt. As if they deserved that. As if the choice of supporting a monster didn't warrant an equally vitriolic reaction.

We were supposed to understand their "economic anxiety" and not further brand them as deplorables, despite their vote securing such tagging. Of course, they each loved to highlight that some of those people voted for Obama, the political equivalent of "I can't be racist because I have a Black friend." For some, perhaps it makes a charming bedtime story, but the reality is, to vote for Barack Obama does not mean you cannot be racist. Racists have lain down with those they hate, and the second they pull their pants up, they're right back to putting those they view as less-than back in their place. A vote is nothing. The man they voted for is a bigot. If you vote for a racist candidate, you are either an unabashed racist or you are complicit in racism. The other immediate talking point relates to caution. That the republic would survive because our institutions are stronger than any one man. Of course America will survive in the wake of a win for bigotry; bigotry is what birthed and has long nurtured her.

For the few Black celebrities who lent their support to him be-fore or after the election—Omarosa, Kanye West, Tina Campbell of Mary Mary, Jim Brown, and Steve Harvey, to name a few—I'm as disgusted with them as I am embarrassed. Steve Harvey has at least acknowledged that he should have listened to his wife, Marjorie, and not gone to meet with him. In theory, I understand why Harvey went to talk with him, but, as I imagine his wife made clear, that devil can't deliver anything to Black folks but grief and pain. Yes, leave it to a Black woman to know better—eh, minus the reality-TV villain and Mean Mary of Mary Mary, anyway.

It is remarkable how inept the administration has been. In the nascent period of this crock of an administration, very little has been done to remedy the circumstances that helped him ascend to power. No one wants to own up to their roles. Only a minuscule number of folks in the mainstream media want to have an honest discussion about how pervasive prejudices are in America. And then there is the man himself, who is relentlessly rancorous and has plenty of energy to stay that way despite eating nothing but fast food and well-done steaks with a gallon of ketchup on the side. Evidently, evil makes for a far more potent stimulant than caffeine.

I do worry about us. Us, the marginalized and the oppressed.

The people who don't deserve to suffer even more because far too many white people will put their whiteness ahead of everyone's benefit—including their own. I fear what will happen with all those judges he appoints who will outlast him and chip away at rights we barely enjoy now. I think about the white supremacists with extra pep in their steps in the wake of his political ascension, no matter how disastrously it ends. And I worry about all of us who have to remember with every single tweet from him, every sensationalistic and callous comment made, every poor decision from his administration, and every terribly choreographed cable-news segment in response to them that we are hated that much, and not enough people want to call a thing a thing. I, too, worry about those tasked with covering it all. Like me! Do y'all know how tiring it is to find new ways to say how terrible everything is? How dumb he is? How vile he is? How much of a liar he is? He and his band of nitwits are exhausting on every fundamental level. And it doesn't help that there's a band of political reporters and pundits suddenly realizing that American politics is tribal, angry, and polarized. Where in the fuck have y'all been? A white cloud? Oh, look, I answered my own question. Who will survive Sweet Potato Saddam's America? Hopefully my hair follicles and hairline.

Epilogue: Yeah, Everything Good . . . We Good

*I*n all of the years I have been in New York as an intern, a frequent visitor, or as someone actually paying rent to live in the city, I've been to the Bronx a whopping four times. And, yes, I do feel like I owe Jennifer Lopez a sincere apology. Each time I've gone, though, I've been reminded about some aspect of my past that used to haunt me.

The first time I went was by accident. I might've been paying rent in New York for all of about a month when I hung out with some new friends that I met via Twitter. While drinking sugary drinks that gave me more of a headache than a buzz, I met some boy, quickly exchanged numbers, and, after a few texts, ended up ditching those friends to be with him—which led me to the Bronx. That was me trying to be less rigid about sex and more open to meeting men and enjoying myself.

The second time was impromptu also. A year and change had

gone by, and I was out with friends I'd met the old-fashioned way. One of those said friends brought his boyfriend along whom I found out had a brother who owned a club in the Bronx. He wanted to know if we wanted to keep the party going. I'm not turning down free alcohol on a Saturday night when I don't have any other plans besides obsessing over deadlines or watching Netflix and then mentally punishing myself for not tending to said deadlines first. I could have sworn I had seen that club on an episode of *Love & Hip Hop: New York*, but I'll just say if it was good enough for Trey Songz to show up for an appearance, it was good enough for me. In any event, at the end of the night, I got treated to a bit of nostalgia.

As we exited the club and walked to our Uber, a fight broke out in the middle of the street. One of the men, shirtless, angry, and incredibly attractive, tried to throw something through the car window of the person he was fighting. The car was in the middle of the street. They just . . . decided to fight then and there. The image instantly took me back to Houston, where I saw Teddy, a classmate from middle school who had since transitioned, outside of a gay club fighting her ex-boyfriend. That car was in the middle of the street too, and much like that fine-ass man fighting in the uppermost borough of New York, Teddy somehow found a brick and threw it through her ex's car window. In my mind, I was thinking, "Aww! It's just like home!" On the ride back to my apartment, I thought about how brave Teddy always used to be. Always certain of herself. Never cowered to anyone talking slick. She was always brave that way. It took me a while to be even half as brave.

The next time, I went to the Bronx Museum of the Arts to cover *Art AIDS America*, a traveling exhibition originally cocurated by Rock Hushka and Jonathan David Katz for the *Village Voice*.

The exhibit included some 125 works—paintings, photographs, sculptures, mixed-media pieces, videos, and prints—loosely divided into four categories: Body, Spirit, Activism, and Camouflage. Much of what stuck out to me was one section in particular—Camouflage—focusing on the challenges many artists faced in creating personally relevant work after legislation passed in 1989 that restricted federal funding for art dealing with homosexuality and AIDS. The same goes for the rampant homophobia gay men faced at the time. Facing criticism about the lack of Black artists featured, the exhibit had ended up adding three by the time it reached the Bronx—amounting to a whopping eight. Still, the first thing you noticed in the exhibit was Marlon Riggs's 1989 documentary *Tongues Untied,* which focused specifically on the uniqueness of Black gay identity. I thought about my uncle. I thought of all the gay Black men of my own generation living with HIV. I thought about some of those I knew who had lost their lives in recent years to AIDS. I thought about my paranoia about becoming one of those people. I thought about how I learned to stop allowing that paranoia, that fear of dying, to prevent me from living.

That feeling was with me the next time I went back to that museum to speak at an event organized for gay Black men who had launched their group with the intent to instill a greater sense of community among queer, gay, and bisexual men. I was asked to talk about "creative expression." I assumed they wanted me to talk about writing for a living, but to be blunt, as an essay-hustler whose work is largely made up of responding to awful people and their horrible antics in pop culture and politics, I increasingly find myself exhausted from both the news and humanity. Still, I agreed, because

I felt it was important to be a part of something with that sort of mission—even if I was a bit grouchy.

I had every intention of planning a formal talk, but in actuality, I didn't come up with even a general idea of what it was I wanted to say until minutes before I arrived. Thankfully, they didn't notice. So I just talked about myself and my background. How I initially wanted to be a news anchor and how I kinda fell into writing full-time. How I wanted to write books and be on television and offer a perspective I felt was missing: working class, southern, Black, gay, country, twerk-friendly, and so forth. As I spoke more, I remembered that even in the midst of my frustrations, I did have a purpose: I wanted to make people laugh and make people think. I wanted to write and say things that I hoped would make it better for those who came after me.

And, yes, I talked about my family, religion, boys, and stigmas.

After I finished, someone came up to me and said, "I mean no disrespect I really enjoyed your talk. I will say one word, though: pain." He said "no disrespect" because he worried I would react the wrong way and pop off on him, I guess. I didn't take offense. Why would I?

Shortly before that talk, I had spoken at a panel on the HIV/AIDS crisis in the Black community. In both cases, I was honest about my experiences and forthright about how they impacted me. Some people cried, but I didn't. I didn't need to, because I'm all cried out about that. That's not where my head is anymore. I used to worry so much about coming across as sad. I feared that I would be adding to a lingering narrative about people like me. I learned to stop fixating on that so much. Some parts of my life are sad, but I am not a sad spirit.

As I explained to the guy, "It's fine that you heard pain, but what matters is that I'm able to speak about it without breaking down, and with hope." Even if he didn't want to say it explicitly, I think he anticipated me speaking about my life in a way that ended with a pretty little bow around it. I get it. When people talk about their lives—in speeches, on panels, in memoirs, in documentaries, and the like—you're often given some ending that's packaged that way. You're typically given something that leaves you feeling all warm and fuzzy. I aim to inspire and be inspired, but I don't necessarily have to speak about my life through that kind of filter.

In the past, there were days when I didn't want to get out of bed. I struggled emotionally because I refused to deal with my anger, with my self-loathing, and with my insecurities about my sexuality and so many aspects of my childhood. I would so easily just keep going, and took the approach that I would get back to all that eventually. *Eventually* never came, and I suffered as a result of it. There were times when I tried to convince myself that I was trying to change, but in reality, it was just me talking rather than actually doing.

But I have done the work now. Still, I have a few remaining concerns. I don't know how some things will work out with respect to my folks. I do wish my mom would be like, "I talked to Jesus, and he said it's cool. I mean, I got the sugar, and you got sugar in your tank. It's all good!" But at the same time, whatever happens happens. I am not in control of that.

I don't know what day I'll pay off my damn student loans, but *whew*, how I long for that shit. To that point, every now and then, I worry that I should have taken up escorting as a minor in college to put off these private student loans. It's never too late to mumble rap, though!

And there are moments when I play a certain R & B song and think, "Damn, I'm single as shit. Still!"

Speaking of R & B, as an intern way back in 2003, I met Mary J. Blige. Her *My Life* album has always meant so much to me. It is my all-time favorite album. I have long given it partial credit for keeping me alive and pushing me to work hard so I could thrive and enjoy life. I got to meet her interning at Majic 102 in Houston. She was there to promote her *Love & Life* album, which was better than a lot of y'all gave it credit for. The DJ I worked under, Kandi Eastman, had stepped out of the studio for a second, and Mary entered. It was just me and her.

She entered the room wearing an all-white jacket and a big smile. "Hey," she said. "How you doing?"

Before I could even answer, Mary extended her arms and gave me the biggest hug. Maybe she thought I was the DJ, but who cares? I was hugging Mary without having to post bail as a result.

"I have something I wanted to share with you," I said. "Whenever you find the time to read it."

"Cool," she answered. She placed the letter in her Louis Vuitton bag.

She did the interview, and that was it. I wasn't sure if she'd actually read the letter or if it would just end up in the trash.

Your album was the first album I ever purchased. And I've been playing it nonstop for nine years. Even when I didn't understand every single thing you were talking about, I could feel your sadness, and it helped me cope with my own. You've helped keep me sane and want to keep going.
I know what it's like to feel miserable and unloved, I

know what it's like to have people constantly criticize you,
and I understand what it's like to want to be happy but sim-
ply can't be. I know it's mainly women that admire you. But
I wanted you to know that I, too, appreciate the honesty in
your work and the fact that you've been brave enough to be
so open throughout your career.

A week later, I was in Los Angeles at the Staples Center watching a charity basketball game. During halftime, I picked up my
phone and saw that I had a voice mail.

"Michael, how you doing? This is Mary J. Blige."

My eyes lit up, and I almost fell out of my chair.

"I read your letter finally," Mary said. Her voice was wavering. It
sounded like she wanted to cry. "I just want to say to you. You have
no idea. You made my day.

"You made it to where *I* want to go on. I thank God for you and
this letter. "

I was stunned. She even left a number for me to call her back. When
I called back, her then fiancé, Kendu, answered the phone. I could hear
Mary grab the phone when her soon-to-be husband said my name.

"Hello?" she asked.

"Hey, this is Michael, I'm the one who wrote you the letter . . .
in Houston?"

"Hey, Michael," she said. "I remember you."

"Thank you for taking the time to read my letter," I said.

"No, Michael," she said. "Thank *you* for writing it." She went to
say, "You will find someone just as beautiful as you are."

After that call, I realized I could make a connection with people
through my writing.

I write all that to say, I'm still single, Mary J. Blige. Where is this person you promised? Also: I'm so mad at Kendu. I'll never not be mad. I love you, Queen!

But no, my life isn't perfect. There are still some things I would like to change. However, what *has* changed is that while everything isn't ideal (when is it ever?), I don't worry the way I used to.

It's natural to have moments of doubt, but what keeps us going is faith. When I rejected the religion I was raised in, I struggled, because I didn't formulate any other belief system. That is no longer the case. I do believe in a God, but more than anything, I believe in me. No matter what comes my way and no matter what happens around me, I am going to be okay. I always have been. I always will be.

I was never looking for a happy ending anyway. What I've been longing for is a new beginning. I've settled on the reality that I can't date Jesus, but I can have the life of my choosing.

It took me longer than most to realize that, but I've long been a late bloomer. And better late than never.

Acknowledgments

I love my parents, and while I know my writing this book may not have been their ideal choice, it would have been impossible for me to do it without them. I'm grateful to them as well as my siblings, Nicole and Marcus, my gorgeous nieces, Alexis and Alyssa, and the rest of my family.

Thank you to the immensely talented Helena Andrews for providing me with a template for how to chase this dream. Thank you to the incomparable Denene Millner, who for every year it took for me to get an agent and then a deal, continued to both believe and champion me. You allowed me to have my sad moments, but you always pushed me to keep going, knowing that eventually the world would catch up. I can never say "thank you" enough.

Thank you to my agent, Jim McCarthy, who after calling me into his office to revisit past dialogue, said, "I think I may have made a mistake." I may have not been completely ready, but you certainly made sure that I was and ultimately became just as passionate as me about this journey. Thank you to my editor, Rakesh Satyal, who told me at a coffee shop in Midtown to just be a little patient because he, like Jim, believed in me, and would help make sure this country gay Black boy got to share his story the way he wanted to.

Thank you to Kimberly Milburn, who has listened to me talk about what all I wanted in my career for nearly two decades. I love you, I love your family, and I'm so appreciative of how y'all have treated me since we forged a bond at James Madison Senior High School's Blue and White game at Butler Stadium so many years ago. Thank you to Astrid McClendon for always being an ear because, as you know, sometimes only those who have had experiences like you can relate to what you're grappling with.

Thank you to andré williams, my friend-turned-brother and tour buddy, for your friendship, your ear, and your eternal optimism. I am so glad "Missez" featuring Pimp C brought us together. Thank you to Devon Augustine for being one of the brightest specks of light in my life. As much as I cherish the memory of us of recreating the "No Time" video on an escalator at the Century City Mall after so many margaritas, it doesn't top all the years we have loved and supported each other. Nakisha Williams: I love the shit out of you and am so grateful to you for everything. Thank you to Janet Mock and Aaron Tredwell for being such amazing friends who, like my aforementioned beloved, have come to feel more like family.

Now, this is the part where I want you to hear *all* of this in the voice and delivery of the late Whitney Houston at the first BET Awards: thank you to Sarah Lake, Lauren Ware, Maiya Norton, Charreah Jackson, Jason Parham, Alex English, Kirk Moore, Amber Reece, Raia Eke-Oduru, Brandon and Brian Smith, Mimi Blanchard, Shanise Coatney, Candy Reyes, Jessica Woodson, Xavier D'Leau, Corey Davis, Richard Brookshire, Sade Hazard, David Johns, Nicholas Nelson, Lauren Ball, Marcus Vanderberg, Robert

Vann, Melanie Martin, and Nakea Tyson. I know that I am forgetting a few, and yes, this is the part when you can refer to me as "punk ass bitch." I still love you, though.

I'd be remiss if I didn't acknowledge the people in media who have not only helped me in some way, but have inspired me and/or befriended me: Melissa Harris-Perry, Doreen St. Felix, Clover Hope, Jenna Wortham, Kelley L. Carter, Richelle Carey, Darnell Moore, Bomani Jones, Samantha Irby, Jamilah Lemieux, Kierna Mayo, Pia Glenn, Desus Nice, The Kid Mero, Danielle Henderson, Bevy Smith, Kiese Laymon, Zach Stafford, Ross Scarano, Jermaine Spradley, Rembert Browne, Tracy Clayton, Heben Nigatu, Mitzi Miller, Aliya S. King, Dan Charnas, Tia Williams, Emil Wilbekin, and yeah, I am probably forgetting more people so y'all can cuss me smooth out too. Also, thank you to every editor who has given me work along the way—particularly the ones who've consistently looked out for me.

Once more: if I forgot you, blame my thot and not my heart.

By now I know you are looking for your name, but no, I didn't forget about you, Luis Roberto Machuca. You are undoubtedly one of the most intriguing additions to my life, but regardless of complications, the fact that we annoy each other, and general uncertainty, I couldn't have finished this book without you. I hope my impact on you has been at least half as strong as the one you've had on me.

And as I wrap this shit up, shout out to Hiram Clarke. I am who I am because of where I come from and what all I've experienced. To that end, to everyone reading this for one reason or another, who has some person, some institution, or some combination of the two trying to break you, allow me to quote one of my favorite singers, Teedra Moses: "Be yourself and if you people don't fool with it, fuck them."

Oh yeah, and Mo'Nique, too, 'cause *I love us for real.*

About the Author

Michael Arceneaux is a Houston-bred, Howard University-educated writer currently living in Harlem. Covering issues related to culture, sexuality, religion, race, and Beyoncé, Michael has written for the *New York Times*, the *Guardian*, *New York Magazine*, Complex, The Root, *Essence*, and many other publications. Additionally, he's lent his commentary to MSNBC, VH1, NPR, Viceland, and SiriusXM, among others.